RIVALS IN THE RING

15 Greatest Boxing Rivalries of All Time

ANDREW DALZIEL

.

"His mouth made him feel like he was gonna win. Not his hands. I had my hands. He had his lips."

- Joe Frazier on Muhammad Ali

CONTENTS

INTRODUCTION

In no sport can individual rivalries be so intense as in boxing. There is something almost primeval about standing in the ring together, with the ultimate aim of either knocking out or stopping their opponent, often with a crowd baying for blood.

Sometimes these rivalries have spilled over outside the ring. While there can be an element of circus attached to professional boxing, there was no element of pantomime when it came to Jack Britton's dislike towards Ted Lewis, for example, or the real hurt that some of the taunts of Muhammad Ali caused Joe Frazier.

At the same time, it should never be forgotten that boxing can also be a profoundly dangerous sport. Benny Paret lost his life in the ring after one fight, whilst two bit-players in the Chris Eubanks – Nigel Benn story were left with life-changing injuries.

And that is without mentioning the later impact on individual health of a career spent being hit for a living. Ali, Frazier, Floyd Patterson, and Ingemar Johansson would all fall victim to forms of dementia in their old age.

Advances in medical science mean that fighters nowadays would not be allowed to fight each other with the frequency that a pair like Sam Langford and Harry Wills did.

It may be the Sport of Kings – and increasingly of Queens – but that does not always make it noble and true.

Ultimately, any compendium of boxing rivalries is left with the difficult choice of what to include and what to leave out; those that follow can be regarded as an exemplar of many more.

MUHAMMAD ALI V JOE FRAZIER

The Louisville Lip v The Smoking Joe

Name	Cassius Marcellus Clay Jr. (later changed his name to Muhammad Ali)	Joseph William Frazier
Height	6 foot 3 inches (191 cm)	5 feet 11.5 inches (181 cm)
Weight	Light heavyweight, heavyweight	Heavyweight
Hometown	Louisville, Kentucky	Beaufort, South Carolina
Nickname(s)	The Louisville Lip, The Greatest, The People's Champion	Smokin' Joe
Overall Career Record	61 fights – 56 wins, 5 losses	37 fights – 32 wins, 4 losses, 1 loss
Head to head	2 wins, 1 loss, 0 draws	1 win, 2 losses, no draws
Style	Orthodox	Orthodox
Recognition	WBA, WBC, The Ring, NABF and NYSAC heavyweight champion, Olympic gold medallist	WBA, WBC, The Ring and NYSAC heavyweight champion, Olympic gold medallist

Arguably the rivalry between Muhammad Ali and Joe Frazier is not only one of the biggest of all-time in boxing but also one of the greatest ever between two individual athletes. It encompassed three fights that took both men to the very limits of their physical and mental capabilities and produced so much heat and rancour that it is still remembered today.

Even those far too young to have seen either man in his prime will forever bracket the two together.

MUHAMMAD ALI

Muhammad Ali was born Cassius Clay in Louisville, Kentucky (one of his numerous nicknames was the '*Louisville Lip*').

He began training as an amateur boxer at the age of 12 and six years later won gold in the light heavyweight division at the 1960 Olympics in Rome. He turned professional later that year before converting to become a Muslim the following year (he later changed his name to reflect this).

Moving up to heavyweight, he boldly predicted he would beat the reigning champion Sonny Liston when they met in the ring in 1964. He followed up that boast by defeating Liston by a technical knock-out, a major upset at the time. The fight was characterised by Ali taunting Liston both before and during the fight, setting the tone for his behaviour for much of his career.

Ali was the best heavyweight in the world for the next three years, but his reign ended when he refused to be drafted to fight in the Vietnam War. The boxing federation stripped him of all his titles, and he was sentenced to five years in jail, although he remained free whilst his case was appealed.

JOE FRAZIER

Frazier had enjoyed a sparkling amateur career, winning the Golden Gloves heavyweight championship in three successive years between 1962 and 1964. He earned himself a late call-up to the American squad for the Tokyo Olympics after an injury to the original first-choice pick.
He went all the way to the final where, despite going into the bout with a broken left thumb that he hid from everybody (including his trainer), he beat Hans Huber of Germany to win the gold medal.

He turned professional the following year and soon hooked up with Eddie Futch, one of the most respected trainers in boxing at the time.
Frazier soon gained a reputation for his punching power, earning himself the nickname '*Smokin' Joe*', and with Ali out of the way fighting his legal issues; he soon became a leading contender for the heavyweight crown.

He first claimed the title when he beat Jimmy Ellis for the vacant WBA title at Madison Square Garden after Ellis' trainer Angelo Dundee (the same man who stood in the corner for Ali throughout almost the entirety of his career) refused to let his man come out for the fifth round to avoid further punishment.

A defence against light heavyweight champion Bob Foster followed before he was ready to face Ali for the first time.

THE ORIGINS OF THE RIVALRY

The two were not natural enemies.

Frazier, in fact, had a great deal of sympathy for the situation that Ali found himself in and had initially refused to fight for the WBA crown because he had considered it unjust to strip Ali of his title.

He had even helped the former champion, giving him a lift from Philadelphia to New York in his car, discussing plans about their first fight and envisaging how much money they could make from it, which left Frazier with the impression that they had become friends.

However, when they got to New York, the other side of Ali showed itself.

He leapt out of the car, announcing to bystanders, *"Smokin' Joe, he's got my title. I want my title! He ain't the champ. He's a chump! I am the people's champ!"*

At the time, Frazier just laughed it off as banter, and he even petitioned the US President at the time, Richard Nixon, to help get Ali's licence back.

However, despite the fact that Ali had not fought since 1967, many boxing fans considered him the true champion because he had not been beaten in the ring. In addition, he was also considered a hero of the anti-establishment movement at the time because of his opposition to the Vietnam War, which was becoming increasingly unpopular among Americans.

Frazier was depicted as a defender of the established order, a supporter of the war, and an *Uncle Tom* (an offensive term to describe a black man considered to be excessively servile to white people).

It, therefore, became a contest between ideologies, as much as sport, compounded by the fact that the two men did not like each other.

DID ALI MEAN IT?

In retrospect, it is difficult to judge how much Ali's taunting of Frazier was real and how much was part of the hype he used to describe himself and belittle his opponents.

What is true, though, is that they got through to Frazier and hurt him emotionally, leaving him with tremendous hatred and resentment towards a man he had once admired. Being told you are ugly and stupid repeatedly can do that to a person, and the 'Uncle Tom" slur was particularly resented in the circles in which he moved (nor was there any merit to the accusation).

Frazier said before their first fight, *"He called me an Uncle Tom. For a guy who did as much for him as I did, that was cruel.*

"I grew up like the black man. He didn't. I cooked the liquor. I cut the wood. I worked the farm. I lived in the ghetto.
"He betrayed my friendship.
"I sat down and said to myself, I'm gonna kill him. Simple as that. I'm gonna kill him."

Ali probably just saw it as part of his armoury and charm, a routine that was expected of him by his fans.

But it also helped define the narrative both at the time and in the eyes of history.

Because Ali was always much better at self-publicity than Frazier, he has come to be depicted as the good guy in this tale and Frazier the villain, which was never the case.

A CONTRAST IN STYLES

The two men had vastly contrasting styles. Ali relied on speed, agility and footwork, dancing around the ring and picking off his opponent with long-range jabs as he sought an opening. Frazier, who was shorter, preferred to get closer, pounding the body before unleashing a destructive left hook.

THE FIRST FIGHT

The first fight between the pair, labelled *'The Fight of the Century'*, occurred in March 1971 at Madison Square Garden in New York.

Ali, with just a couple of warm-up fights behind him after his reinstatement, came out fighting with a flurry of shots and won the first two rounds, but then Frazier caught him with a left hook, signalling that he would not fold easily.

Frazier and Futch had devised a tactic based on Ali's tendency to throw a right uppercut from a straight standing position. Frazier was instructed to throw a left hook at the time when he sensed Ali's head would be immediately afterwards.

The two traded blows through the middle rounds, and the pair were even on most scorecards going into round 11.

But then the fight's momentum changed when another hook from Frazier sent Ali crashing into the ropes. The defending champion put the result beyond doubt when he dumped Ali on the canvas in the 15th round, only the third time in his career he had been knocked down.

It was the first defeat of Ali's career.

The fight was watched by a then-record 30 million people globally, with each fighter taking home a purse of US $2.5 million.

THE REMATCH

Two years later, Frazier lost his title when he was beaten by the young and upcoming George Foreman, suffering a technical knock-out defeat, having been sent to the canvas six times by the younger man.

He set about regaining his title, but, first of all, there was the no small matter of a rematch with Ali.

The second fight, a non-title 12-round fight, occurred at Madison Square Garden in January 1974.

The bad blood between the two had continued when they appeared together on a TV show five days before the fight, hosted by sports commentator Howard Cosell.

Initially, it had begun cordially, with Ali declaring, *"I don't hate Joe Frazier, Joe Frazier don't hate me,"* but then the former champion could not help himself and began to call Frazier ignorant and stupid.

Frazier took objection to the jibes made by Ali, confronted him, and the pair started grappling before their two entourages separated them.

In the fight itself, probably the least memorable of the three encounters between the pair, Ali again began on the front foot. However, as the fight went on, he started to engage in new tactics, using a half-hook uppercut from both sides and resorting to frequent clinching, holding his opponent behind the neck with one hand whilst using the other to prevent Frazier from deploying his vaunted left hand. As a result, Frazier was precluded from working his body or using the left hook, denying him some of his most potent weapons.

Ali was judged the winner by a unanimous decision, and he had his revenge, although many boxing commentators were unhappy with the tactics he had used.

THE THRILLER IN MANILA

A year later, Ali had won back the title in dramatic fashion, knocking out the champion George Foreman in the *'Rumble in the Jungle'* in Zaire, Africa, using the *'roper dope'* tactic for seven rounds before springing into decisive action.

The venue for the third fight in the trilogy was Manila in the Philippines. Ali had arrived in the country like a conquering hero and was pictured in public, whilst Frazier headed to the mountains to train in solitude.

Ali engaged in his usual rhetoric before the fight, famously taunting his opponent, *"It will be a killer and a chiller and a thriller when I get the gorilla in Manila"*.

The fight began at 11 am local time so that it could be shown on prime TV in America. That meant conditions were oppressively hot, with temperatures well above 100 degrees Fahrenheit inside the arena. Both men soon became dehydrated, adding to the physical toll the fight took.
If the first two fights had been punishing, this was of a different magnitude altogether, as the pair swapped blows, although Ali did not hesitate to hold Frazier when the referee allowed it.

The pair traded punches, and as it got towards the end of the fight, both men were almost out on their feet, although Frazier appeared in the worse condition, with both his eyes swollen.

The 14th round proved decisive as Ali rained such a devastating range of blows to the opponent's head that some thought they might have been fatal to Frazier.

At the end of the round, Ali had had enough and asked trainer Angelo Dundee to cut off his gloves, signalling that he was finished.
Dundee refused, which, in the event, proved fortuitous.

In the other corner, trainer Eddie Futch was increasingly concerned for his fighter's safety. Frazier could hardly see, was behind on the scorecard, and had barely landed a blow in anger against the champion for the past few rounds.

He made the momentous decision to throw in the towel, despite Frazier's protests, telling him, "*Joe, you've had enough.*"

Shortly before he died, Futch was asked why he stopped the fight with only three minutes left, and he always answered that he was not a timekeeper but a handler of fighters and, in his opinion, Frazier could take no more.

It was a close-run thing, though. Dundee said that Ali was not a quitter, but he had never seen his man so exhausted before, whilst Ali later claimed that he had never been closer to death than in that fight.

Afterwards, Ali said, "*I'll show you any other fight, but not that one. I don't want to see hell again.*"

He also paid tribute to Frazier, saying, "*I always bring out the best in men I fight, but Joe Frazier, I'll tell the world right now, brings out the best in me. I'm gonna tell ya, that's one helluva man, and God bless him.*"

THE AFTERMATH

Arguably both men were never the same after that fight in Manila. Frazier never won a fight after that, being knocked out by Foreman for a second time and then returning to draw with Floyd Cummings in his last fight before hanging up his gloves.

Ali would fight ten more times, but his once considerable powers were waning, with his speed and reflexes blunted, and he lost three out of his last four fights.

LATER LIFE

By the end of his career, Ali was judged to have suffered over 200,000 blows to his face and body. In 1984, he was diagnosed with Parkinson's syndrome, which is often associated with head trauma.

Although he remained active throughout the rest of his life, he was in declining health until he died in 2016.

Frazier went on to train fighters at his gym in Philadelphia, although he walked with a limp following injuries he sustained in a car accident. He was diagnosed with liver cancer in 2011 and died from complications of it soon afterwards.

YEARS OF RESENTMENT AND THEN RECONCILIATION

After that fight in Manila, Ali called up Frazier's son Marvis, a teenager then, and asked him to tell his father, "*Tell your dad the things I said I really didn't mean.*"

Frazier's response was: "*He should come to me, son. He should say it to my face.*"

In old age, Ali reflected, "*I said a lot of things in the heat of the moment that I shouldn't have said. Called him names I shouldn't have called him. I apologise for that. I'm sorry. It was all meant to promote the fight.*"

Both men mellowed as they got older and reconciled before they died. Marvis Frazier explained: "*In the end, before my father passed away, he and Ali came together in love and unity.*

"*I was so happy to see that. They hugged and embraced. That was fantastic.*"

THE LEGACY

In popular mythology, Ali is often considered the hero of the piece and Frazier, the bad man, but it was much more nuanced than that and did not reflect how Ali played the race card to his advantage.

Ali also frequently used humour to downgrade his opponents and did not always mean anything personal by it.

Frazier took it to heart, and, even after he was long retired, continued to hate Ali for some of the things he said about him, although the two men finally found some mutual peace before the end of their lives.

At the same time, there was a core of mutual respect, especially after that third fight in Manila.

It remains one for the ages.

Interesting Quotes

"I always bring out the best in men I fight, but Joe Frazier, I'll tell the world right now, brings out the best in me. I'm gonna tell ya, that's one helluva man, and God bless him."

- Ali on Frazier

"Ali even told me in the ring, 'You can't beat me - I'm your Lord.' I just told him, 'Lord, you're in the wrong place tonight."

- Frazier on Ali

SUGAR RAY LEONARD V ROBERTO DURÁN

Sugar Ray v Hands of Stone

Name	Ray Charles Leonard	Roberto Durán Samaniego
Height	5 feet 10 in. (186 cm)	5 feet 7 in. (170 cm)
Weight	Welterweight, light middleweight, middleweight, super middleweight, light heavyweight	Super featherweight, lightweight, light welterweight, welterweight, light middleweight, middleweight, super middleweight
Hometown	Wilmington, North Carolina	El Chorrillo, Panama
Nickname(s)	Sugar Ray	Manos de Piedra (Hands of Stone)
Overall Career Record	40 fights – 36 wins, 3 losses, 1 defeat	119 fights – 103 wins, 16 losses
Head to head	3 fights – 2 wins, 1 loss	3 fights – 1 win, 2 loss
Style	Orthodox	Orthodox
Recognition	WBC and The Ring welterweight champion, WBC super-middleweight champion, WBC light heavyweight champion Olympic gold medallist	WBA, WBC middleweight champion, WBA, WBC super welterweight champion, WBC and The Ring welterweight champion. WBA, WBC and the Ring lightweight champion

Sports historians regard the 1980s as one of the golden ages of boxing thanks to the rivalry between four men who became known as the "Four Kings" – Sugar Ray Leonard, Roberto Durán, Marvin Hagler, and Thomas Hearns.

They helped revitalise a sport that had undergone a fallow spell after the retirement of Muhammad Ali and helped define the decade as they had nine Championship fights between them.

The four of them were not afraid of meeting each other, of putting their reputations and records on the line – they just wanted to get in the ring and fight.

Sugar Ray Leonard and Roberto Durán met each other three times, and whilst the third fight may have been an anti-climax, the first two were anything but.

SUGAR RAY LEONARD

Ray Charles Leonard was born in 1956 in North Carolina before the family migrated to Washington, DC and then Maryland.

He got into boxing first via his older brother Roger, who had joined a local club and won some trophies. Wanting to emulate his brother's achievements, Leonard took up the sport. He soon began to be called Sugar Ray after the legendary former champion Sugar Ray Robinson.

He soon outstripped his brother Roger and became a successful amateur boxer. He was part of the US team for the 1976 Olympics in Montreal, where he was picked as their representative in the light welterweight division.

He won all six bouts, including the final, 5 – 0, when he decided his boxing career was over, saying, *"I'm finished... I've fought my last fight. My journey has ended, and my dream is fulfilled. Now I want to go to school."*

Though fate intervened when he discovered his girlfriend was pregnant and that he was being sued for child support. Without any other means of raising money and with his parents both ill, Leonard decided to become a professional boxer.

Angelo Dundee, Muhammad Ali's trainer, was brought in as his trainer and manager, and soon Leonard began to make headway in the sport, winning his first 25 fights, 16 of them by knockouts.

In 1979 he fought and beat Wilfred Benítez for the WBC Welterweight Championship at Caesar's Palace. A successful defence against the British challenger Dave 'Boy' Green followed, and next up was Durán.

ROBERTO DURÁN

Roberto Durán was born in Panama in 1951. Raised in a slum district, he began boxing in a local gym when he was eight.

He had a successful amateur career before turning professional when he was just 16 years old.

As a lightweight, he won his first 31 fights and, in 1972, became the WBA Lightweight champion, although there was an element of controversy about how he beat his opponent, Ken Buchanan, with suggestions of a low blow as the pair grappled.

Several successful title defences followed although he did suffer his first professional loss in a non-title fight with Estaban de Jesus. He avenged that defeat and became the undisputed Lightweight Champion before deciding to move up to Welterweight.

By the time he was ready to meet Leonard for the first time, he had already had several successful bouts in the category.

Durán, who acquired the nickname 'Hands of Stone', was fearless and had earned a reputation as somebody to be avoided.

In 2016, he said, *"Fighters would take one look at me and then crap in their pants. In many ways I was Mike Tyson, before Mike Tyson came along."*

Age has subsequently mellowed their rivalry and they have both collaborated on a documentary looking back on their fights.

THE ORIGINS OF THE RIVALRY

The rivalry came about because of a clash of cultures.

Leonard was a darling to the American people, having won that Olympic gold medal and was considered to have the brightest future in the sport.

Meanwhile, Durán had fought his way out of poverty and became a symbol of the Panamanian people, synonymous with their triumphs and disasters.

In many ways, it was a David and Goliath struggle, with Durán, at least in the eyes of some of his supporters, cast in the role of the underdog.

THE BRAWL IN MONTREAL

The pair first met in the Olympic Stadium in Montreal, a venue deliberately chosen by Leonard because it was where he had won Olympic gold four years earlier.

Durán resented that he was earning just a fifth of the total prize money, but he soon had other things to worry about.

Three days before the fight, a medical check-up revealed a heart abnormality, which might be associated with coronary artery disease in an average person. However, after more tests, he was cleared to fight by specialists.

Leonard would claim that he was affected by a virus, although Angelo Dundee claimed he did not know of it.

The bout took place in front of more than 46,000 people, and although Leonard had been banking on a warm reception from them, Durán enjoyed the lion's share of support.

For the 15 rounds, they went toe to toe, slugging it out, although the manner of the contest was more to the liking of Durán than Leonard. He could both throw and land more punches, cutting much of the ring off from his opponent.

Leonard went against the advice of Angelo Dundee in his corner, who told him to move from side to side and avoid getting caught on the ropes, saying, *"I will not run."*

Later in the fight, Leonard made some adjustments and began to claw back some of the deficit.

However, Durán had built up such a big score on the judges' scorecards that meant it was a unanimous points decision in his favour at the end.

"I've never been hurt so much in my career," Leonard revealed.

"His fists felt like rocks. ... He hit me so hard so many times in so many places that I looked at him and said, 'You know what? This is it.' I contemplated in the ring that this would be my last fight."

Durán was asked if Leonard was the toughest fighter he had faced, replying, *"Si, si. He does have a heart. That's why he's living."*

NO MÁS FIGHT

The rematch took place just five months later, the timing dictated by Leonard, who knew that Durán could be relied on to party hard after his victory in the first bout.

He later recalled, *"My intention was to fight Duran as soon as possible because I knew Duran's habits. I knew he would indulge himself, he'd gain 40–50 lbs and then sweat it off to make 147 (pounds)."*

His prediction proved right – Durán went on an extended binge, put on a lot of weight, and then was forced to take emergency measures to make welterweight for their second meeting.

Meanwhile, Leonard had trained intensively and was in excellent shape by the time they stepped in the ring together at the Superdome in New Orleans in November 1980.

He had also decided to change his tactics. Whereas in the first fight, he had opted to stay still and trade blows with his opponent, he used his speed and movement this time round, staying out of range of Durán's fists as much as possible whilst looking to score freely.

It proved very effective, and he began to build a substantial lead as Durán started to labour. By the seventh round, Leonard began to taunt Durán, shuffling around the ring, dropping his hands, and even sticking his tongue out at the man from Panama at one stage.

Then, as a reminder of his punching power, he caught the champion full in the face with a left jab before resuming the goading.

The eighth round produced the moment that gave the fight its name.

With Durán taking more punishment, he decided he could not take any more. He turned to the referee and said, *"no más"* and quit the fight. Leonard had won by technical knockout.

The decision took his trainers by surprise, and two of them, Freddie Brown and Ray Arcel, left his team on the spot.

Brown said, *"I was shocked. There was no indication that he was in pain or getting weak,"* whilst Arcel did not mince his words, *"That's it. I've had it. This is terrible. I've handled thousands of fighters and never had anyone quit on me. I think he needs a psychiatrist more than he needs anything else."*

Durán ascribed his decision to the fact that he had begun to suffer from stomach cramps, the result of overeating food post the weigh-in, after his abstinence from the previous weeks.

Leonard was triumphant, *"I made him quit…to make a man quit, to make Roberto Duran quit, was better than knocking him out."*

He later denied ever hearing Durán say "no más."

The damage to Durán's reputation proved to be immense and long-lasting. His popularity in the USA and back in Panama declined, and he lost lucrative advertising deals.

THE THIRD FIGHT

It would be another nine years before the pair would meet for a third and final time. By now, both had moved up the weight divisions, and Leonard was defending his super middleweight title for the second time.

Leonard was now 33 and Durán 38, and whatever expectations fans had ahead of their clash at the New Mirage Hotel in Las Vegas, they were to be disappointed.

Though 16,000 fans bought tickets, and millions more watched on pay-per-view, both men were past their best.

Nonetheless, Leonard was able to use his tactical superiority to beat a lacklustre Durán for a unanimous points decision. However, the challenger did have the satisfaction of cutting the American badly in the 11th round.

It was no spectacle, though; both men were booed during the fight.

THE AFTERMATH

Although the third leg of the trilogy proved to be an anti-climax, their rivalry is best remembered for the two fights that preceded it.

Dúran would have a career spanning five decades and won World Championships as Light Middleweight, Middleweight and Super Middleweight, but his standing within the sport would never fully recover.

Leonard, meanwhile, established himself as the best boxer of his generation and beat the other two of the Four Kings – Marvin Hagler and Thomas Hearns in a series of bruising fights.

In 2016 he was voted the greatest living fighter.

He was the first boxer to earn in excess of US $100 million in prize money.

LATER LIFE

Leonard worked as a boxing analyst for many years but has also appeared in numerous television shows and movies. He has made a fortune from advertising deals and is now a highly sought-after motivational speaker in the United States and overseas.

In addition, he is heavily involved in charitable work, with the issue of juvenile diabetes a particular cause for which he campaigns.

Post-retirement, Durán had the five world title belts he won stolen from his house in Panama in a plot orchestrated by his brother-in-law, who sold them to a memorabilia collector. They were later recovered. He, too, has enjoyed a television and movie career and is currently a brand ambassador for a bottled water company.

Both men have been inducted into the Boxing Hall of Fame.

THE LEGACY

Leonard and Durán are best remembered as part of the Four Kings that dominated boxing in the 1980s and helped keep interest in the sport alive following Ali's retirement. Their first two fights were memorable in different ways, and whilst Leonard went on to have a much better career, that was not necessarily predicted at the time.

Some critics have argued that Durán quitting that time back in New Orleans did him some good in the end because it made his subsequent comeback all the more creditable.

INTERESTING QUOTES

"I made him quit...to make a man quit, to make Roberto Duran quit, was better than knocking him out."

- Sugar Ray Leonard on Roberto Duran

"He does have a heart. That's why he's living."

- Roberto Duran on Sugar Ray Leonard

RIDDICK BOWE V EVANDER HOLYFIELD

Big Daddy v The Real Deal

Name	Riddick Lamont Bowe	Evander Holyfield
Height	6 feet 5 inches (196 cm)	6 feet 2.5 inches (197 cm)
Weight	Heavyweight	Light heavyweight, cruiserweight, heavyweight
Hometown	Brooklyn, New York	Atmore, Alabama
Nickname(s)	Big Daddy	The Real Deal, The Warrior
Overall Career Record	45 fights – 43 wins, 2 losses	57 fights, 44 wins, 10 losses, 2 draws, 1 no contest
Head to head	3 fights – 1 win, 2 losses	3 fights – 2 wins, 1 loss
Style	Orthodox	Orthodox
Recognition	WBA, WBO, WBC, IBF Heavyweight Champion	WBA, WBF, USBA, WBC Heavyweight champion, WBA and IBF Cruiserweight champion

Between 1992 and 1995, Riddick Bowe and Evander Holyfield fought a trilogy of heavyweight fights that were to rival those of Muhammad Ali and Joe Frazier. Bowe emerged the overall winner over his former sparring partner, but after the last fight, the two men's careers headed in opposite directions.

Holyfield would go on to become the only four-time world champion, whilst Bowe retired relatively early, having failed to live up to his earlier potential. In retrospect, his fights with Holyfield were the highlights of his career.

RIDDICK BOWE

Born in New York in 1967, Bowe was in the same elementary class as Mike Tyson but later claimed: *"I really didn't know him."*

He began boxing as a teenager and had a successful amateur career, winning the prestigious New York Golden Gloves Championship four times, initially as a light heavyweight and then, after he gained 30 pounds, as a super heavyweight.

Despite not initially being part of the squad for the US Olympic team for the Seoul Olympics, he was eventually chosen. He reached the final but had to settle for a silver medal after losing a controversial fight to Lennox Lewis, representing Great Britain.

Soon after, he turned professional and came under the wing of legendary trainer Eddie Futch (famous for his association with Joe Frazier). Futch also claimed that Bowe had more potential than he had ever seen in any other fighter.

After a series of fights, including two against Elijah Tillery, he had put himself in contention to fight for the World Championship.

EVANDER HOLYFIELD

Born in Alabama in 1962, Holyfield began boxing at seven but was a late developer physically and would only grow to his full height in his early 20s.

He earned a bronze medal at the Summer Olympics in 1984 after being disqualified in his semi-final bout and turned professional as a light heavyweight earlier that year.

Holyfield moved up a weight to Cruiserweight and soon became world champion, mounting several successful defences of his title. He had loftier ambitions and moved up a weight again to challenge for the world heavyweight title.

He soon became the number one contender for the title that Mike Tyson held at the time, but instead fought Buster Douglas after the latter produced a major surprise by knocking out Tyson in Tokyo.

Holyfield was Douglas' first title defence, but the challenger knocked him out to take his title.

He then beat former champion, George Foreman. By the time he was ready to face Bowe for the first time, he was undefeated.

THE ORIGINS OF THE RIVALRY

The rivalry between the two sprang from the fact that they were both leading heavyweight contenders at the time. There appears to have been nothing personal between the pair. In fact, they were friendly towards each other, having previously sparred.

SPARRING PARTNERS

They sparred together when Holyfield was the cruiserweight champion and Bowe was still an amateur. Holyfield later recalled, "*Bowe was a young guy, but he was always bigger than me …. he was trying to take me out. I was tearing him up [in sparring], and I was asking myself, 'How in the world does this guy think [he can take me out?"*

THE FIRST FIGHT

The first fight between the two took place in Paradise, Nevada, in November 1992.

Holyfield went into the contest a clear favourite despite the challenger having a 30-pound advantage. Still, the champion found it challenging to land his punches against the bigger, stronger, younger man.

By the start of the tenth round, Bowe was ahead on the scorecards, and he looked to press home his advantage with a furious assault on Holyfield that visibly hurt the champion.

However, Holyfield summoned his inner resolve, survived the barrage and dominated the second half of the round, landing some combinations of his own.

That took its toll on Holyfield, and Bowe dominated the 11th round and scored a knockdown. Despite announcer Jim Lampley claiming it would be "a miracle" if Holyfield got up, he did just that and mustered a sustained attack in the final round to try and save his title.

That proved in vain, and Bowe won by a unanimous decision to claim the title. Holyfield had suffered the first defeat of his career.

THE FAN MAN FIGHT

The pair met again a year later for a rematch overshadowed by one of the most bizarre incidents in the history of boxing.

With the pair evenly matched in the seventh round, many in the crowd began looking upward, and some started yelling and running for cover. Holyfield recalled, "*I heard this weird sound from somewhere up above, like a vacuum cleaner or something.*"

It was actually a grown man, James Miller, attached to a parachute, attempting to paraglide into the ring as a stunt. He misjudged his approach, his chute got tangled in the lights, and he landed on the apron of the ring and the ropes.

Bowe's entourage quickly pulled him from the ropes, beating him with their mobile phones until he was unconscious. Meanwhile, Bowe's pregnant wife fainted and had to be taken to hospital by ambulance.

The intervention of 'Fan Man' had a potentially pivotal effect on the outcome of the fight.

The judges had to score the seventh round, and the confusion may have impacted their verdicts because one gave it to Bowe, another to Holyfield, and the third Morse Jarman had it even.

Had Jarman given the round to Bowe, the overall fight would have ended in a draw (Bowe had begun the fight strongly), and the champion would have retained his title. As it was, though, it was Holyfield who won a narrow points decision and had the title back again.

Miller claimed that he landed in the fight because he was opposed to violence, although his younger brother later said his motivation was to buck society.

He would go to try and interfere with an NFL playoff game and was deported by the British authorities after serving a short prison sentence for interrupting a Premier League game between Bolton Wanderers and Arsenal.

In his most famous stunt, he landed in the Mall in London in front of Buckingham Palace, removing his trousers to reveal that he was painted green from the waist down. He was deported again.

THE FINAL CHAPTER

After their Nevada fight, Holyfield had lost his heavyweight crown to Michael Moorer despite a second-round knockdown and had retired soon afterwards with a heart condition that he later claimed was misdiagnosed.

He made his comeback to the ring in 1995. Bowe, meanwhile, had fought four times and won all his fights. The pair agreed to a third non-title bout that was dubbed 'The Final Chapter'.

Unlike the previous two fights that had gone the distance, this proved to be the most brutal of all their contests, with Holyfield not at his best, suffering the side effects of hepatitis A.

By round five, he seemed exhausted but defied his physical condition in the next round by sending Bowe sprawling to the canvas with a left hook to the chin. It was the first time Bowe had been knocked down in his professional career.

Bowe responded with two knockdowns of his own in the eighth round, only for Holyfield to show all the courage for which he was renowned. This time, though, Bowe responded by knocking him down again with a short right hand, and although Holyfield was able to beat the count, he was quickly knocked down again, causing the referee to stop the fight.

THE AFTERMATH

Despite that defeat, Holyfield would go on to have much the better subsequent career of the two.

Holyfield continued his comeback, eventually earning a highly lucrative rematch with Tyson, whom he knocked out in the seventh round. He became only the second heavyweight after Ali to win the world title more than twice.

He retired as the only four-time world champion.

Bowe had several more fights, including two against the Pole Andrew Golota, that were mired in controversy, with Golota disqualified on both occasions.

He then briefly quit the sport altogether to join the Marine Reserve Corps, only to have a change of mind after three days.

He returned to the ring and had three more bouts before hanging up his gloves.

The talks about a fourth fight with Holyfield were held, but it never came to anything.

Bowe never really fulfilled his potential, mainly because he did not train seriously, particularly towards the end of his career. Arguably he was never better physically than when he fought Holyfield and was a shadow of his former self by the end of his career.

However, he was also the first fighter at any weight to hold all four versions of the world title.

He always held high regard for himself, saying, *"The thing is this sport doesn't have a heavyweight who is prettier than I am"* and *"I mean, who at my best could give me a good fight?"*

LATER LIFE

Bowe had a troubled private life away from the ring and suffered legal, personal and financial problems for years. He spent time in jail for kidnapping his estranged wife and their five children and briefly contemplated a career in professional wrestling.

In 2015 he was inducted into the International Boxing Hall of Fame.

Holyfield would continue boxing until he was 50 and, at one point, wanted to fight the Klitschko brothers. By his own admission, he said, *"Fighters find it hard to give up doing what they do best – fighting for a living."*

However, he decided to retire, and although he was scheduled to take part in several exhibition bouts, these have failed to materialize.

There have been allegations that he used steroids and performance-enhancing drugs during his career, although he has always denied this, and the claims have never been proven.

Like Bowe, he has been inducted into the Boxing Hall of Fame.

THE LEGACY

Although their rivalry was fierce, there was always a degree of mutual respect between the two. Their trilogy of fights was marked by drama and excitement, leaving a lasting legacy in the sport of boxing

INTERESTING QUOTES

Bowe would say of his opponent, "*Man. I'm gonna tell you something about Evander Holyfield, when he fights a guy like me, and I fight a guy like him, we always bring the best out of each other so by no means should anyone think that a fight like that is a cake walk because it's not.*"

As for Holyfield, he clarified his feelings about Bowe, saying, "*Riddick was a good fighter — a real good fighter. He could fight inside and outside. He wasn't just a big puncher; he was a skillful fighter, he had the jab, and he boxed very well. Bowe was more of a challenge than pretty much all of them except [Mike] Tyson. Any time I fought Bowe, I knew it was going to be a tough fight. The only person who ever had my heart racing as fast as that was Tyson.*"

JAKE LAMOTTA V SUGAR RAY ROBINSON

The Bronx Bull v Sugar

Name	Giacobbe LaMotta	Walter Smith Jr.
Height	5 feet 8 inches (173 cm)	5 feet 11 inches (180 cm)
Weight	Middleweight, light heavyweight	Lightweight, welterweight, middleweight, light heavyweight
Hometown	Manhattan, New York	Alley, Georgia
Nickname(s)	The Raging Bull, The Bronx Bull	Sugar
Overall Career Record	106 fights – 83 wins, 19 losses, 4 draws	201 fights – 174 wins, 19 losses, 2 draws, 2 no contests
Head to head	6 fights – 1 win, 5 losses	6 fights – 5 wins, 1 loss
Style	Orthodox	Orthodox
Recognition	NBA, NYSAC, and the Ring middleweight champion	NBA, The Ring and NYSAC middleweight and welterweight champion

Over the course of nine years, Jake LaMotta and Sugar Ray Robinson fought each other six times in a series that culminated in a bout that became known as the '*Saint Valentine's Day Massacre*'.

Five of their fights went the full distance, with intensity unrivalled before Muhammad Ali and Joe Frazier got in the ring together.

LaMotta is best remembered today for his portrayal by Robert de Niro in the film '*Raging Bull*'. He specialised in close in-fighting and blows to the body, whilst Robinson was nimbler on his feet, trying to pick his spot to land combinations and looking for the knockout blow.

Whilst they may have had contrasting styles, both were feared, and others would shy away from fighting them – one of the reasons they ended up fighting each other so often.

There was a good deal of respect between the pair. LaMotta would later say, "*I fought Sugar Ray so often, I almost got diabetes*", and "*The three toughest fighters I ever fought were Sugar Ray Robinson, Sugar Ray Robinson, and Sugar Ray Robinson*".

JAKE LAMOTTA

Born in the Lower East Side of New York, LaMotta began fighting at an early age thanks to his father, who encouraged him to fight other boys to entertain neighbourhood adults, who would throw money into the ring which was used to pay the family's rent.

He learned to formally box in reform school, which he had been sent to for attempted robbery.

Fighting as an amateur, he went unbeaten as a middleweight before turning professional at the age of 19.

He won 14 out of 15 of his first bouts before a trilogy against Jimmy Reeves, which saw him defeated in the first two but emerge the winner in the third.

By this time, he had already acquired the reputation of being a slugger — not a particularly big puncher. He would stalk his opponents around the ring, aiming to get inside and inflict vicious beatings on them. He was also known as '*The Bronx Bull*'

His turbulent private life included connections with the mob and issues with his temper, which saw him almost beat a man to death during a robbery.

He was married seven times but later admitted to beating several of his wives and raping another woman.

SUGAR RAY ROBINSON

Robinson was born in Georgia as Walker Smith Jr but moved to New York after his parents separated. Growing up, he wanted to be a doctor but switched to boxing after dropping out of high school.

Initially, he was told he was too young to enter his first boxing tournament, but he got around this by using the ID card of a youth called Ray Robinson, who had decided to quit the sport.

He began fighting under that name, adding the sobriquet after a lady in the audience described him as '*sweet as sugar*' at one of his fights.

He had an outstanding amateur career, finishing with a record of 85 − 0, with 69 knockouts, 40 of which came in the first round.

In 1940, at 19, he turned professional and was undefeated by the time he was ready to face LaMotta for the first time.

THE ORIGINS OF THE RIVALRY

There was no personal animus between the two men. They fought so often because contests between the pair were always such good box office, and promoters knew they could profit from them.

Their sixth fight, for example, was one of the first to embrace the use of television as a promotional tool, and, beyond those lucky enough to watch it in the flesh, it was seen by several million sat in their living rooms.

THE FIRST FIGHT

Their first meeting came in October 1942 at Madison Square Garden in New York, in Robinson's first fight as a Middleweight, having stepped up from Welterweight for the occasion.

Although Robinson (145 pounds) was the lighter man in comparison to LaMotta (157.5 pounds), he managed to control the fight despite suffering a first-round knockdown. He picked himself up, ensured he did not let his opponent get too close again, and landed the harder punches himself.

He claimed a unanimous decision from the judges.

THE SECOND FIGHT

The rematch came just four months later in Detroit, with Robinson again the lighter man going into the bout, which was scheduled for ten rounds.

For the first part of the fight, Robinson dominated proceedings with his lightening quick hands and seemed to be on the way to another decisive points win.

However, in the eighth round, a desperate LaMotta came to life and managed to get inside his man, applying relentless pressure. He finished the round with a right to the body, following up with a left hook to the head, which sent Robinson through the ropes.

The bell saved him from being counted out, and he survived the last two rounds, but LaMotta had assumed control of the fight by now, and he handed Sugar the first defeat of his professional career.

It would be another nine years and 91 fights before Robinson was beaten again.

THE THIRD FIGHT

LaMotta would be given little time to savour his victory because they met for the third time just 21 days later.

It was another close fight, and LaMotta knocked his man down again in the seventh round. Robinson beat the count when it reached nine. Robinson later said, "*He really hurt me with a hook in the seventh round. I was a little dazed and decided to stay on the deck.*"

However, using his left jab and uppercuts effectively, Robinson won another unanimous decision.

LaMotta was unhappy with the decision, claiming that it was only awarded to Robinson because he was going into the army the next day (he himself was excused from military service because of a childhood operation on one of his ears which affected his hearing).

THE FOURTH MEETING

It would be another two years before the pair met again, this time back at Madison Square Garden.

Widely regarded as the least interesting of all their fights, it ended with Robinson again winning by a unanimous decision. Some at the ringside even awarded him nine out of the ten rounds.

FIGHT NUMBER FIVE

The fifth meeting between the two, which took place at Comiskey Park in Chicago in September 1945, was by far the most controversial. Robinson won by split decision, with both men bruised and bloodied at the end, much to the annoyance of the nearly 15,000 fans in attendance, who booed vociferously when he was announced the winner.

Several newspapers and boxing publications opined that the decision should have gone in favour of LaMotta, whilst Robinson later acknowledged afterwards that *"This was the toughest fight I've ever had with La Motta"*.

THE SAINT VALENTINE'S DAY MASSACRE

Having met so frequently in such a short time, it would be another five years before they met again.

In the meantime, Robinson finally won the World Welterweight title in 1947, whilst LaMotta claimed the middleweight crown in 1950.

However, with Robinson increasingly finding it hard to make the weight limit, he moved up to middleweight, setting up a sixth meeting between the pair with the world title on the line.

It took place in Chicago on February 14th, 1951, and became known as the Saint Valentine's Day Massacre in homage to the gangland hit ordered by the mobster Al Capone in the same city in 1929.

Perhaps aptly, the mob tried to get involved this time, with a famous hitman, Frankie Carbo, approaching Robinson in person, suggesting that the two men should have three fights.

"I want you and the Bull to have three title fights," Carbo continued. "You'll *win the first. He wins the second. The third is on the level."*

"You mean I take a dive in the second?" Robinson fired back with disgust. *"You got the wrong guy."*

Going into the fight this time, LaMotta struggled to make the weight and realised he probably lacked the stamina to go the total distance. So bad were his issues that, some days in the lead-up, the only sustenance he took was in the form of ice cubes.

Given his problems, LaMotta changed tactics, eschewing his usual strategy of relentlessly stalking his opponent to target the head of Robinson more in the hope of knocking him out.

Robinson's corner, though, was aware of LaMotta's weight problems and advised him to box accordingly, which he did by targeting hooks into the ribs and belly of the champion in a bid to sap his energy.

LaMotta's big opportunity came in the sixth round when he caught Robinson with a left hook and followed that up with a combination attack that drew blood and forced Robinson into retreat.

However, the challenger weathered the storm and bided his time, so by the 11th round, La Motta knew he was in trouble. Summoning up his last reserves of energy, he mounted a last-ditch effort and tried to force a stoppage, driving Robinson into the ropes with a non-stop barrage of shots.

The gamble failed, and by the end of the round, he felt the effects of some of the counter-attacks Robinson had launched on him.

As the bell rang for the 12th round, LaMotta had nothing left to give, and Robinson could score at will. Hooks, uppercuts and swinging blows rained down on the champion, and the referee refrained from intervening, perhaps out of respect for LaMotta's reputation as somebody who had never been knocked down.

At the end of the round, the ringside doctor visited LaMotta's corner, but he allowed the fight to continue.

The 13th round was memorable, though not for the right reasons. With LaMotta barely able to keep his hands up by this stage, Robinson launched an almost endless series of attacks, which the referee allowed to continue for far too long. Only raw courage kept LaMotta standing, but when Robinson landed a vicious right-hander that would have sent nearly every other boxer to the floor, the ringside officials decided that he had suffered enough punishment and signalled to the referee to stop the fight.

By the end, LaMotta could barely stand and was half-carried to his corner by his handlers. It was another 20 minutes before he could hobble to his dressing room.

THE AFTERMATH

LaMotta was never the same fighter again.

He made the decision to move up to light heavyweight but struggled for results at first, and by 1954, he had decided to retire from the sport.

Meanwhile, Robinson went on a European tour, during which he lost his world middleweight title to the British boxer Randolph Turpin before winning it again in a rematch.

In 1952, he suffered the only knockout of his career in a fight with light heavyweight champion Joey Maxim, although the extreme heat in the ring may have had something to do with it.

He retired soon afterwards, but two and a half years later made a comeback and regained the world middleweight title in 1955.

He became the first boxer to win a divisional world championship five times, and in 2021, he was ranked as the greatest pound-for-pound boxer of all time.

LATER LIFE

After he retired, LaMotta owned and managed a bar in Miami Beach, and it was whilst there that he was arrested on charges of introducing men to an underage girl. He was convicted and served six months on a chain gang whilst continuing to protest his innocence.

He also pursued an acting career, appearing in more than 15 films, and testified to a US Senate sub-committee looking into the underworld's influence on boxing. He confessed to throwing one fight so the mob would organise a title bout for him.

Inaugurated into the Boxing Hall of Fame in 1990, he died of pneumonia complications at the age of 95 in 2017.

Robinson did not retire until 1965, by which time he had spent the entire US $4 million he had earned in his career inside and outside of the ring.

Like LaMotta, he had some acting roles and helped create a Foundation for the Los Angeles inner-city area. He then contracted Alzheimer's and died aged 67 in 1989.

The Legacy

Inevitably their rivalry is best remembered from the Raging Bull movie and Robert de Niro's portrayal of LaMotta (for which he won the Oscar for Best Actor).

The film takes some liberties with the truth. At the end of the Saint Valentine's Day Massacre scene, LaMotta utters, "*You never put me down, Ray. You never put me down,*" whereas, in reality, he was too battered and exhausted to say anything.

However, it remains one of the great sports, let alone boxing, movies of all time, depicting not just the brutality of the sport and some of its protagonists but also the courage and sheer grit of those who choose to make a living from it.

Interesting Quotes

"The three toughest fighters I ever fought were Sugar Ray Robinson, Sugar Ray Robinson, and Sugar Ray Robinson"

- Jake LaMotta on Sugar Ray Robinson

"You mean I take a dive in the second?. You got the wrong guy."

- Sugar Ray Robinson when asked to fixed a fight with LaMotta

SAM LANGFORD V HARRY WILLS

Boston Tar Baby v The Black Panther

Name	Samuel Edgar Langford	Harry Wills
Height	5 feet 6.5 inches (169 com)	6 feet 2 inches (188 cm)
Weight	Lightweight, welterweight, middleweight, light heavyweight, heavyweight	Heavyweight
Hometown	Weymouth Falls, Nova Scotia	New Orleans
Nickname(s)	Boston Rat Baby, Boston Terror, Boston Bonecrusher	The Black Panther
Overall Career Record	314 fights – 210 wins, 43 losses, 53 draws, 8 no contests	111 fights – 89 wins, 10 losses, 7 draws
Head to head	17 fights – won 2, lost 6, drew 9*	17 fights – won 6, lost 2, drew 9*
Style	Orthodox	Orthodox
Recognition	World welterweight and world heavyweight champion	Denied the chance to fight for world titles because of his colour

* These numbers are open to some dispute

Most boxing rivalries are based on one or two fights between two contenders. What is remarkable about the rivalry between Sam Langford and Harry Wills is that there were at least 17 fights between them, with some sources claiming that it may have been as high as 22.

Wills won six of them, Langford two, but the remainder finished with no result, indicating how closely matched the two men were.

The uncertainty surrounding the number of times they fought each other and the lack of comprehensive details about their fights can be attributed to the racial dynamics of the era. Both individuals involved were African-American, and the predominantly white press of that time did not extensively cover their bouts. Consequently, this limited coverage and racial bias contribute to the disputed accounts and incomplete information surrounding their encounters.

SAM LANGFORD

Langford has been described as 'The greatest boxer you've never heard of', mainly because he is black and was active in an era when racial segregation was still in full force in the US. Many white fighters refused to fight coloured opponents, whilst most venues barred integrated matches.

It meant talented black heavyweights were denied the opportunity to fight for the official world title, instead being forced to fight each other numerous times for unofficial championships.

For example, although Jack Dempsey is widely regarded as one of the greatest heavyweights of all time, he never stepped in the ring with a black opponent.

Not that Langford, who went by various nicknames '*The Boston Tar Baby*', '*The Boston Terror*' and the '*Boston Bonecrusher*', started out as a heavyweight.

He was only five feet seven inches tall and, after a troubled early life, was offered a job as a janitor in a boxing gym. He soon found himself pressed into action as a sparring partner for local fighters before taking up the sport himself.

He soon became the Featherweight champion of Boston and then stepped up to beat Joe Gans, considered one of the greatest Lightweight Champions of all time.

He continued to progress up the weight divisions and would go on to win the unofficial World Coloured Heavyweight Championship five times between 1910 and 1918, a record.

Despite his small stature, he boasted clever footwork, fast hands, and potent combination punching, which enabled him to knock out much bigger men.

HARRY WILLS

Like Langford, Wills was a victim of the prevailing colour bar of the time. Known as the '*Black Panther*' and standing six feet four inches tall, Wills had a muscular body due to working long hours as a longshoreman and was known for his tremendous punching power.

Of his 75 professional victories, 47 were by knock-out, and in 2003 Ring Magazine included him in their list of the 100 hardest punchers of all time.

THE ORIGINS OF THE RIVALRY

Why did they fight each other so often?

Because they were denied the opportunity to fight white boxers, fighters like Langford and Wills were forced to settle for frequent bouts among the ranks of other talented coloured fighters of the time.

Langford, for example, also fought Joe Jeanette 14 times, Jim Flynn on six occasions, Jack Johnson 12 times, and Sam McVey 15 times.

There is no suggestion that Langford and Wills had any personal animosity towards each other – this was just a job, after all, and a way of earning money.

THE FIRST BOUT

The pair first met in May 1914 when Langford was the unofficial heavyweight champion while Wills was the upcoming young challenger. The much taller and heavier man, Wills, emerged from the fight with a draw, although some neutral observers believed he should have won it on points.

THE SECOND FIGHT

It was the first rematch between the pair six months later in Vernon, California, for the Coloured Heavyweight Championship, which is best remembered.

By that point, Langford was a 31-year-old veteran with 158 fights behind him, having faced every fighter imaginable in every weight class. Wills was the younger man by six years – not even did he have age on his side, but he also had the greater reach, strength and, in the eyes of many observers, the greater punching power.

He may have lacked some of the ringcraft of his more experienced foe but had become a fine boxer in his own right.

A large crowd gathered to watch the fight scheduled for 20 rounds.

Wills, though, was determined that it should not last that long and sought to dominate the much smaller man from the opening bell, dropping Langford to the canvas four times in the opening two rounds.

Langford, though, had a strong chin and courage in abundance, and he got up each time, even though he picked up an ankle injury that impaired his movement in the first part of the fight.

But Langford was resilient and had courage in abundance, and he responded with a knockdown of his own before the fight settled into an attritional battle, with no quarter asked or given.

Wills was able to keep Langford at arm's length initially with long straight punches, but as he began to tire, the smaller man was able to close the gap and get to work inside. He was also helped by his ankle gradually loosening up, which helped both his footwork and his balance.

Suddenly the momentum shifted in favour of Langford as he landed some telling blows on the challenger.

Going into the 14th round, Wills was still ahead on the scorecards, but that soon became irrelevant.

What happened next is open to dispute.

Wills later claimed that he had been in control of the round and had backed Langford into a corner when, out of the blue, Langford produced a left hook that dropped him to the canvas. Wills could not get up in time.

However, a newspaper report at the time said that Langford had worn him down before producing a combination that was finished off by the left hook.

Some observers believed that Wills' lack of experience ultimately cost him dear and that Langford had used his tenacity and wisdom to get the better of him.

Not that Langford emerged from the fight scot-free. Not only did he have the ankle to contend with, but he had suffered eye damage during the encounter.

LATER FIGHTS

The following year, Langford lost his heavyweight title to Jeanette, and his career began to decline, although he would continue to fight Wills periodically. He beat Wills for the second – and final - time in February 1916, but thereafter, the younger man would have the better of things.

LATER LIFE

Langford began to suffer from eyesight problems as he got older, compounded by a detached retina during a bout with Fred Fulton in

1917. Five years later, he suffered damage to his remaining good eye in a fight with Tiger Flowers, but barely able to see, he still managed to put his man down with a powerful shot to the head.

Although the '*Boston Tar Baby*' was urged to quit the sport, he continued fighting because he was broke and needed the money, even becoming the Mexican Heavyweight champion in 1923. However, he had to rely on his cornermen to guide him into the ring.

His final fight at the age of 43 was stopped on the grounds he was unable to see his opponent.

He retired near destitute until a sportswriter for the New York Herald Tribune located him and published a tribute soliciting enough donations to enable him to see his final days in a private nursing home in Boston.

Shortly before passing away in 1956, he became the first non-world title holder to be inducted into boxing's Hall of Fame.

Wills went on to have a fine career, even though he was denied the chance to fight for the world title because of the refusal of Dempsey to get in the ring with him. Instead, he had to be content with fighting other coloured fighters, which even white boxing commentators at the time considered to be an injustice.

He ended his career at 43, but, having invested what he had earned in his career wisely, enjoyed success in the real estate business in New York and ended his life in prosperity.

He, too, was inducted into the Boxing Hall of Fame in 1992 and is regarded by some as one of the finest fighters never to have held the world heavyweight title.

THE LEGACY

Their legacy extends beyond their in-ring battles. Wills and Langford were trailblazers in a time when racial barriers heavily influenced the sport. As African-American fighters, they faced significant challenges and discrimination, often encountering limited opportunities and biased media coverage. Despite these obstacles, they persevered and became symbols of resilience and excellence.

Their rivalry shattered stereotypes and proved that talent and determination transcend race. Wills and Langford inspired future generations of boxers, particularly African-Americans, who aspired to greatness in the sport. Their fame helped pave the way for greater inclusion and recognition of black fighters in the boxing world.

INTERESTING QUOTES

"You'll pardon me gentlemen if I make the fight short. I have a train to catch."

- Sam Langford

"The greatest boxer never to fight for a world title."

- Harry Wills was once described as the greatest boxer to never fight for the title after Jack Dempsey denied him the title shot because of his colored skin

-

TONY ZALE V ROCKY GRAZIANO

The Man of Steel v The Rock

Name	Anthony Florian Zaleski	Thomas Rocco Barbella
Height	5 feet 9 inches (175 cm)	5 feet 7 inches (170 cm)
Weight	Middleweight	Welterweight, middleweight
Hometown	Gary, Indiana	Brooklyn, New York
Nickname(s)	Man of Steel	The Rock, Rocky, Rockaby
Overall Career Record	87 fights – 67 wins, 18 losses, 2 draws	83 fights – 67 wins, 10 losses, 6 draws
Head to head	3 fights – 2 wins, 1 loss	3 fights – 1 win, 2 losses
Style	Orthodox	Orthodox
Recognition	NBA, NYSAC, The Ring middleweight champion	NBA, NYSAC, The Ring middleweight champion

In less than three years, Tony Zale and Rocky Graziano had a trilogy of fights that have gone down in the annals of boxing historians because of their ferocity and sheer brutality.

In contrast to styles, no quarter was asked or given when 'The Rock' took on 'The Man of Steel'.

So good were their fights that two of them were named "Fight of the Year" by Ring Magazine, although none went even half the distance.

Yet, for all their rivalry in the ring, there was nothing personal about it, and after they had finished fighting each other, they became lifelong friends.

TONY ZALE

Zale was born in 1913 in the steel town of Gary, Indiana, which was partly responsible for him giving his later nickname.

At the tender age of two, Zale's life took a tragic turn when his father met a devastating end in an accident. It was an incident that haunted him for years, burdening him with the weight of self-blame. On that fateful day, Zale's father hopped on his bicycle to get medicine from a nearby drugstore for ailing Tony. Tragically, a collision with a car proved fatal, leaving Tony's world shattered, robbed of a beloved father.

Growing up shy and introverted, Zale soon began working in one of the local steel mills, despite his tender age. He later recalled complaining to his brother as he walked through the factory gates, "*I feel like I was born here*", only to be told in reply, "*Stop bitchin'. Be thankful you got a job.*"

He began boxing in a local gym, where a coach stopped him and said, "*You look like you're made out of steel*". From there on, he adopted the nickname '*Man of Steel*', which he kept for the rest of his life.

He turned professional in 1934, but without any immediate success, he returned to working in the mills before trying again three years later.

This time he stuck with it, and in 1940 he won the National Boxing Association middleweight title. He had acquired a reputation as a fearsome fighter, with one opponent commenting, "*When Zale hits you in the belly, it's like someone stuck a hot poker in you and left it there.*"

In 1941, he fought Georgie Abrams for the world Middleweight title, and, despite being knocked down in the first round, he fought back and won the fight narrowly on points.

The following year he lost a non-title fight, but then his boxing career was put on hold due to the war, and he served in the US Navy.

By the time the war finished and he was ready to resume his career, he was 33 years old and probably past his prime.

ROCKY GRAZIANO

So colourful was Graziano's life, especially in his early years, that it later became the subject of an award-winning Hollywood movie, '*Somebody Up There Likes Me*', starring Paul Newman.

Brought up in a rough part of New York, the son of an occasional bareback rider, he started boxing at three. His father kept boxing gloves in the house and encouraged Graziano to fight his older brother almost every night.

He endured a difficult childhood. Rocky was frequently beaten by his father and joined a street gang, where he soon found himself in trouble with the law and spent years in and out of reform school.

At 18, he became an amateur welterweight champion, but, despite the potential prize money and fame that went with it, he had no interest in becoming a professional boxer at that stage because of the discipline and training required.

Weeks into his amateur career, he was arrested again for stealing and incarcerated in a correctional facility with another future champion, Jake LaMotta. He never fought him in the ring, though, later claiming, "*Why should I fight Jake, I always liked him in reform school.*"

He began boxing again to earn money but soon found himself detained again for a probation violation and was sent to Rikers Island.

This time he enrolled in the army when he got out, but found military life not to his liking and went AWOL after punching a captain. This time he began boxing professionally under the name 'Rocky Graziano'. He won his first few fights and started making a name for himself.

Unfortunately for him, the military authorities caught up with him, and he was court-martialled. He was given a dishonourable discharge and sent to a federal penitentiary, where he resumed his boxing career.

He was eventually pardoned. Graziano still did not like training much, but he produced a major upset when he knocked out Billy Arnold at Madison Square Garden in March 1945.

By the time he was ready to face Zale for the first time the following year, he was 26 years old.

THE ORIGINS OF THE RIVALRY

Their rivalry only came about because they fought each other three times in such a short space of time, and there was no personal animosity between the pair. In later life, they became close friends and appeared in TV interviews together.

The two men had contrasting styles. Zale was considered the polished one, relying on the jab to work his opponent's body and wearing them out before delivering the knock-out punch.

Graziano became known for his ability to absorb a tremendous amount of punishment before unleashing a devastating punch that saw him win many fights via knockdown.

THE FIRST FIGHT

Zale won his six bouts after coming out from the Navy, but by the time he was ready to face Graziano for the first time, many considered him to be past it, and his chances in the lead-up to the fight were not helped when he contracted pneumonia.

Graziano was considered the favourite when they met at the Yankee Stadium in New York in September 1946, but it was he who ended up on the canvas first when Zale put him down for a count of five in the opening round.

However, he came back and dropped Zale at the end of the second round, who got up on the count of three.

Graziano continued to pound away savagely at the body of Zale, who appeared to be beaten, especially as he had damaged his hand in the second round.

However, in the sixth round, Zale found some inner resolve and hit Graziano in the solar plexus with a right, and after Graziano got back to his feet again, Zale followed that up with a left hook to the chin.

Graziano failed to beat the count this time and had to be propped up as he was led around the ring.

Years later, looking back at the footage of the fight again, Graziano said, "*After that body shot that knocked me down, I was out on my feet. The referee should have stopped the fight, then. I didn't even know where I was.*"

Meanwhile, ringside commentators observed that "*Zale was so battered from the punches of Graziano, by the end of the fifth, he mistook his opponent's corner for his own. Fans yelled for referee Rudy Goldstein to stop the fight, but the veteran official allowed the fight to continue.*"

Graziano described Zale as "*Tougher and faster than anybody I ever fought in my life.*"

THE SECOND FIGHT

There was an immediate clamour from boxing fans for a re-match, originally scheduled for New York in February of the following year, only for Graziano to be suspended by the New York State Athletic Commission for failing to report an attempted bribe.

His suspension was lifted in time for him to face Zale again, this time in Chicago in July 1947.

This time it was Zale who dominated the early rounds. Graziano suffered a cut over his eye in the second round and was knocked down in the third. With his right eye also beginning to swell, the fight was in danger of being stopped.

Sensing that his chance was slipping by and barely able to see, Graziano unleashed a furious attack in the fifth round, hitting Zale with a flurry of blows that left the champion badly hurt.

Only the bell saved him, but the respite proved to be temporary.

Graziano pursued him all across the ring in the sixth round, backing Zale into the ropes and hitting him repeatedly. With the champion half in and out of the ring, referee Johnny Behr had seen enough and stopped the fight.

The new champion then uttered the immortal line, "*Hey Ma, your bad boy done it.*"

THE THIRD FIGHT

Graziano would hold the middleweight belt for almost a year before the two met for the third and final fight between two in June 1948 in Newark, New Jersey.

In a fight that was every bit as brutal as the first two meetings, Zale knocked Graziano to the canvas in the first round. In the second, Graziano was hurt by a right hand from Zale but responded with a big right of his own.

Then in the third, Zale dropped Graziano again with a left hook and, after he got up on the count of seven, knocked him out cold with a left hook to the jaw.

In the process, Zale became the third Middleweight boxer to regain the World Championship.

THE AFTERMATH

Zale's wife wanted him to retire after the final Graziano fight, but he held on for one more payday, this time against the French champion Marcel

Cerdan in Jersey City. It proved a step too far, as Cerdan, cheered on by his lover and famous singer Edith Piaf, took his title off him in 12 rounds.

Shortly after their final fight, Graziano was suspended by the NBA (now WBA) indefinitely for pulling out of a scheduled fight, with the ban applied worldwide to all fights under their jurisdiction. He was eventually reinstated and continued fighting until 1952 but would never again become embroiled in such a battle as he had with Zale.

Later, he would admit to having nightmares that he was back in the ring again with Zale.

SOMEBODY UP THERE LIKES ME

Graziano's story became the subject of a book and then a movie starring Paul Newman (replacing James Dean, who was killed in a car accident).

Still in good shape, Zale almost played himself, but the idea was eventually shelved.

Unfortunately, Zale always did have trouble pulling punches. He kept knocking Newman out!

Meanwhile, when it was rumoured that Frank Sinatra wanted to play the lead role, Graziano apparently dismissed the idea saying, "*Frank, you're too skinny to play me.*"

LATER LIFE

Zale worked as an amateur boxing coach in Chicago on a part-time basis but shied away from publicity and did his best to avoid reporters eager to discuss his sporting past. However, he was always ready to contribute when his good friend Graziano was involved.
He later contracted Parkinson's and Alzheimer's disease and spent his last years in a nursing home. He died in 1997.

Meanwhile, Graziano co-hosted a television show briefly and was a regular in several other series. He also appeared in numerous television commercials, later remarking that he made far more money doing it than he had ever earned in the ring.

He also appeared as a boxer in a 1967 film, '*Tony Rome*' and owned a string of pizza restaurants and a bowling alley in New York. He died in 2009.

Both men were inducted into the Boxing Hall of Fame in 1991.

THE LEGACY

The enduring rivalry between Rocky Graziano and Tony Zale remains an iconic chapter in boxing history. Their epic battles captivated fans, showcasing their relentless styles and unwavering determination. From Zale's initial victory to Graziano's revenge and, finally Zale's redemption, their trilogy of fights defined an era.

Their clashes were marked by fierce competitiveness, mutual respect, and legendary displays of skill and resilience. The Graziano-Zale rivalry left an indelible mark, representing the essence of boxing at its finest. Even today, their thrilling encounters are remembered as a testament to their enduring legacy and the impact they had on the sport.

INTERESTING QUOTES

"Tougher and faster than anybody I ever fought in my life."

- Zale on Graziano

"I never stole nuttin' unless it began with an 'A' - A truck, a car, a payroll...!"

- Rocky Graziano

TED LEWIS V JACK BRITTON

The Aldgate Sphinx v The Boxing Marvel

Name	Gershon Mendeloff	William J. Breslin
Height	5 feet 7.5 inches (171 cm)	5 feet 8 inches (173 cm)
Weight	Light heavyweight, middleweight, welterweight	Welterweight
Hometown	London	Clinton, New York
Nickname(s)	The Aldgate Sphinx, The Kid	The scrapper, The Boxing Marvel
Overall Career Record	301 fights – 232 wins, 46 losses, 23 draws	345 fights – 237 wins, 60 losses, 43 defeats, 5 no contests
Head to head	20 fights – 7 wins, 9 losses, 4 draws	20 fights – 9 wins, 7 losses, 4 draws
Style	Orthodox	Orthodox
Recognition	World welterweight champion, British and European middleweight champion	NBA and NYSAC welterweight champion

In an era when boxers may fight several times a year at best, with none of those contests going beyond 12 rounds, it is hard to believe that it was once not uncommon for boxers to fight multiple times in the space of 12 months, often against the same opponent. Furthermore, some of those fights could last for as long as 20 rounds and, in some cases, more.

That was certainly the case between Ted '*Kid*' Lewis and Jack Britton, who fought each other 20 times in six years, passing the world welterweight title between them.

Britton is credited with having the better head-to-head record, but this should be taken with a certain amount of salt. No video footage of any of their bouts survives, and their fights were often presented as exhibition matches, with newspapers passing verdicts on the decision the next day.

What is beyond doubt is that the fights were always extremely competitive and that, at least on the side of Britton, there was real animosity towards his opponent.

TED LEWIS

Ted Lewis was born Gershon Mendeloff in London in 1893, the son of a cabinet maker with a Jewish heritage. One of his older brothers had boxed under the name of Lou Lewis, and Ted himself was encouraged to take up the sport by a police officer who had witnessed how he had performed in a street brawl.

He began boxing at 14 at the Judean Athletic Cup, where he competed for sixpence and a cup of tea. However, if he won, he would go home with five pence, as he gave a penny back to cover the cost of the tea.

He adopted the fighting name 'Kid' Lewis (adding Ted later once he got to America) and started appearing in the club's weekly Sunday show.

At the age of 16, he turned professional, but his career did not get off to the most auspicious start as he lost his first fight (either to Johnny Sharpe or Kid Da Costa, as sources vary on this).

By the time he was 17, though, he had become both British and European flyweight champion and, having successfully defended his title, broadened his international appeal by fighting in Australia and Canada before heading for the United States.

One thing that made Lewis stand out was that he was an early proponent of using a mouthpiece called a Gumshield at a time when few fighters went into the ring wearing one.

Despite his physical disadvantage, Lewis would win nine titles ranging from flyweight to the middleweight divisions and would even fight and beat heavyweights. Mike Tyson, an aficionado of boxing history, opines, *"Lewis would win bouts in all eight boxing divisions of his time."*

JACK BRITTON

Jack Britton was born in Clinton, New York, in 1885 and began boxing in local clubs in Milwaukee. He turned professional in 1904 but for some time languished in the lower ranks, and his career was going nowhere until he teamed up with manager Dan Morgan, who insisted that his fighters lived clean and trained hard. Under his guidance, his career began to take off.

Britton was not a hard hitter, but he was quick on his fight, elusive and hard to hit. He has over 350 fights in his career, but he was stopped only once, and that was in just his second fight.

Known as 'The Boxing Marvel', Britton had already fought a trilogy of fights with another Hall of Famer, Packey McFarland, when he faced

Lewis for the first time. His first bout with McFarland ended in a draw, whilst there were No Decisions in the other two, but all three fights were praised for the artistry in the ring shown by both men.

THE ORIGINS OF THE RIVALRY

Britton disliked Lewis for several reasons. The first was because he was a Jew. The second was because Lewis was English, whereas Britton was proud of his Irish heritage. Britton's manager Morgan put it thus, "*Britton was Irish, and so was I. Could we trust an Englishman?*"

After Britton beat Lewis on St. Patrick's Day in 1919, he even sent a telegram to King George V at Buckingham Palace boasting that somebody Irish had beaten an Englishman.

Lewis also had a reputation as a dirty fighter in some quarters, with many of his fights ending in disqualifications.

For whatever reason, Lewis did not like Britton either, refused to speak with him and chose to forego the usual handshakes between the fights.

At a time when many fights were known to be fixed, the public appetite for clashes between the two was insatiable because they knew that what they were seeing was above board and honest.

THE FIRST FIGHT

In early 1915, Britton defeated Mike Glover to establish his claim to the world welterweight title. When Lewis also beat Glover, the stage was set for the two to meet for the first time.

Lewis had changed his style by the time he arrived in America. Previously he had tended to shift from side to side, relying on his long left jab, but he evolved into a fighter who would swarm his opponents, throwing rapid-fire combinations, a style that made him popular with the public.

The bad blood between the two was evident even before the first bell had rung, but in a wild bout, Lewis got the decision and became the champion.

Lewis had become the first English fighter to cross the Atlantic and beat an American on home soil to a world title. And in the process, he also became the youngest world champion in history.

THE OTHER FIGHTS

The pair would have exclusive rights to the world welterweight title for the next six years, passing it back and forth, even though many of them were non-title fights.

There were three meetings in 1915, five in 1916, five in 1917 (including four in less than two months), four in 1918, and two in 1919. Their final bout was in 1921.

Their meeting on St. Patrick's Day in 1919, which occasioned Britton to send his famous telegram, was decisive because the American won by a knock-out after being stopped in the ninth round. Britton had extra motivation because of the holiday.

Later Lewis claimed that he had been sick in the lead-up to the bout and had only taken the fight because he did not believe that Britton had the power to knock him out.

Just before their final meeting in 1921, the referee gave the pair their final instructions in the ring when Britton's manager Morgan objected to Lewis wearing his Gumshield. The New York State Athletic Commission inspector agreed, and Lewis was forced to fight without it.

THE AFTERMATH

Despite many thinking that his best days were behind him after fighting Britton for the final time, Lewis defied expectations by winning both the British and the European middleweight titles.

He then failed in his attempt at the European heavyweight title when a sucker punch by Georges Carpentier controversially beat him. Lewis had been dominating the fight, but when he turned to the referee warning him about holding, the Frenchman knocked him out with a vicious right.

A year after the final Lewis fight, Britton was involved in one of the most controversial bouts of all time when he beat Benny Leonard in New York

City after the latter was disqualified for hitting Britton when he was down in the thirteenth round. The sportswriters who witnessed the bout believed that Leonard had committed the foul deliberately because he did not want to hold two titles, and many of the spectators thought that the fight had been fixed.

Britton lost his welterweight title in 1922 to the much younger Mickey Walker (there was a sixteen-year age difference between the pair), who sent him to the canvas three times. The fight at Madison Square Garden inspired Ernest Hemingway's short story 'Fifty Grand'. Hemingway did not actually attend the fight but was inspired by newspaper accounts of it.

Although he would never again fight for a title, Britton would continue fighting until 1930, finally retiring after losing to Rudy Marshall at 44.

LATER LIFE

During his time in America, Lewis became a celebrity, meeting his future wife and becoming friends with Charlie Chaplin, who would become godfather to his son. He flirted with the movie business but found himself typecast as a boxer.

Returning to England, he became interested in politics. He began to follow the fascist party of Sir Oswald Mosley, going so far as to be given the responsibility of recruiting and training the '*Biff Boys*' who would form an honour guard at Mosley's meetings.

In 1931, he stood for parliament for Mosley's party, but his campaign was a disaster and attracted only 154 votes.

However, when Lewis became aware of the anti-Semitism of Mosley's politics, he began to distance himself, and according to his son, he decided to quit the movement. He argued violently with Mosley and punched several of his bodyguards before knocking out two more guards as he left the building.

Lewis had several occupations in later life, working variously as a boxing trainer, manager and referee, a bookmaker, vintner, haberdasher, travel agent and security officer, as well as making numerous personal appearances.

His association with 'dubious elements' continued as he got to know the infamous Kray twins, Reggie and Ronnie. The gangsters would invite Lewis along to birthday parties and charity events, and he was even used once as a decoy when they sprung a fellow criminal from Dartmoor Prison.

He spent his last years in a Jewish retirement home and died in 1970 at the age of 77. He is regarded as one of the finest pound-for-pound British fighters of all time.

Lewis was elected into the Boxing Hall of Fame in 1964.

Britton lost all the money he made in the ring in failed investments in land in Florida. He became a boxing instructor and mentor to young fighters and also ran a drugstore with his wife in Miami. The Boxing Marvel also had a brief spell as an actor and was a professional wrestler for a while. He died in 1962.

Britton was inducted into the International Boxing Hall of Fame in 1990. Today, he is remembered as one of the finest welterweights ever to have stepped in a ring.

THE LEGACY

The rivalry between Jack Britton and Ted Lewis was intense and enduring, leaving a lasting impact on the sport of boxing. From 1915 to 1921, Britton and Lewis faced each other a remarkable 20 times, captivating audiences with their skill and determination. Their bouts were marked by a stark contrast in styles, with Britton's defensive prowess and counterpunching ability pitted against Lewis' relentless aggression and powerful punches.

Britton and Lewis became iconic figures in the boxing world, drawing large crowds and elevating the sport's popularity during a crucial period of growth. Their fights are still studied and celebrated by boxing enthusiasts and historians, as it showcases the best aspects of the sport.

INTERESTING QUOTES

"Ted Kid Lewis was one of my favorite of all times and the greatest fighter to come out of Britain. Lewis would win bouts in all eight boxing divisions of his time"

- Mike Tyson on Ted Lewis

"Britton was Irish, and so was I. Could we trust an Englishman?"
- Britton's manager on Ted Lewis

FLOYD PATTERSON V INGEMAR JOHANSSON

The Gentleman of Boxing v The Hammer of Thor

Name	Floyd Patterson	Jens Ingemar Johansson
Height	5 feet 11.5 inches (182 cm)	6 feet 0 inches (183 com)
Weight	Light heavyweight, heavyweight	Heavyweight
Hometown	Waco, North Carolina	Gothenburg, Sweden
Nickname(s)	The Gentleman of Boxing	Ingo, The Hammer of Thor
Overall Career Record	64 fights – won 55, lost 8, drew 1	28 fights – won 25, lost 3
Head to head	Won 2, Lost 1, Drawn 0	Won 1, Lost 2, Drawn 0
Style	Orthodox	Orthodox
Recognition	Two world titles – recognised by WBA, NYDSAC, The Ring	One world title – recognised by WBA, NYDSAC, The Ring European heavyweight title Olympic silver medal

When the world heavyweight title was one of the most prestigious in sport, the three fights that Floyd Patterson and Ingemar Johansson fought in less than three years became instant classics.

Yet few gave the Swede any chance when he stepped into the ring with Patterson for the first time, with the American just regarding it as a warm-up bout for bigger and better things.

Hundreds of thousands of Johansson's fellow Swedes stayed up half the night to listen to the fight on the radio, and when he won, it was acclaimed as the biggest sporting achievement in the country's history.

Patterson was to gain his revenge, making his own piece of history in the process, but their trilogy of fights is still watched on YouTube to this day.

FLOYD PATTERSON

Patterson was born to a low-income family in North Carolina in 1935, one of eleven children. When his family moved to Brooklyn in New York, Patterson played truant from school and became a petty thief. At the age of ten, he was sent to a reform school, which he later credited for turning his life around.

A natural athlete, who excelled at all sports, he took up boxing at the age of 14, and three years later, he won gold at the Helsinki Olympics as a middleweight.

He then won several prestigious amateur championships, and legendary trainer Cus D'Amato spotted his talent.

As a professional, although he enjoyed early success in boxing as a light heavyweight, it was always the intention that he would eventually move up a division, and the retirement of Rocky Marciano created a vacancy for the heavyweight title.

Having won a series of elimination fights, Patterson faced Archie Moore, the light heavyweight champion, for the World Heavyweight Championship, knocking him out in the fifth round.

He then had a series of routine defences before he was ready to face Johansson, who had become the number-one contender for the first time.

INGEMAR JOHANSSON

Johansson was born in Gothenburg in 1932 and discovered at an early age that he could fight and had "*thunder in his hands*". He entered amateur boxing and was part of a European team that travelled to take on their American counterparts in 1951, knocking out his opponent in two rounds in Chicago.

The following year he qualified for the Sweden team for the 1952 Olympics in Helsinki, but his campaign there was to end in ignominy. In his final bout with the eventual winner Ed Sanders, Johansson was disqualified by the referee for passivity and not trying hard enough, as he spent most of the fight trying to stay out of the American's reach.

Johansson later tried to justify his performance by claiming that he had enjoyed limited training opportunities and that his trainer had instructed him to let Sanders be the aggressor.

Nevertheless, it cut little ice with the Olympic Committee as they withheld his silver medal; and it would take 30 years before it was restored to him.

Under a cloud, he went into seclusion six months after the Olympics and considered quitting the sport. Instead, under the aegis of Edwin Ahlquist, a Swedish boxing promoter and publisher, he turned professional and won his first 21 professional fights, becoming the European champion.

He earned his shot against Patterson by knocking out the previously top-ranked contender, Eddie Machen, in front of his home fans in Gothenburg.

THE ORIGINS OF THE RIVALRY

Patterson and Johansson were two contrasting figures with different approach to boxing. While Patterson and many other fighters of his day would adopt a strict training regime before fights, Johansson was more of a playboy, not training too hard, and often seen in New York nightclubs with his girlfriend, a writer for Sports Illustrated.

He was later dubbed boxing's equivalent to Cary Grant, and, fittingly, he would appear in a Hollywood movie alongside Sidney Poitier and Alan Ladd. The Swede was known for never appearing in public without a beautiful woman on his arm.

At the same time, as far as Patterson was concerned, Johansson was fighting on his turf in the United States and was after a title he felt was the exclusive preserve of Americans. No European had held the Heavyweight title since Primo Carnera of Italy in the 1930s, and Patterson was in no mood to let the Swede end that drought.

There was no personal animosity, though, and, in later life, they became close friends. They attended boxing conventions simultaneously and were always happy to sign merchandise and memorabilia together.

THE FIRST FIGHT

When they met at the Yankee Stadium in June 1959, Johansson entered the ring as a 5 – 1 underdog. D'Amato recommended that Patterson face the Swede because he was a limited fighter he could easily outbox.

His assessment proved to be completely misplaced.

Not that seemed apparent in the first two rounds as Johansson was happy to stay on the back foot, flicking the occasional left jab at the champion.

But, at the start of the third round, Johansson threw a left hook, which Patterson blocked with his right hand, temporarily opening himself up. Through a short, powerful right, Johansson then set Patterson crashing to the canvas. He got up again, only to be knocked down six more times before the referee stopped the fight.

Ingemar would describe the right hand that accounted for Patterson as the '*Hammer of Thor*', and a New York newspaper headline the next day captured the general air of amazement at the result, declaring '*Ingo – It's Bingo*'.

Johansson would return home to Sweden, a national hero, arriving by helicopter and celebrated wherever he went.

For Patterson, though, he felt humiliated, saying, "*It was bad enough to lose the title, but losing it to a foreigner was even worse.*"

A rematch was on the cards almost as soon as the first fight had ended, with the US public demanding it because they considered that the sporting honour of their country was at stake.

THE SECOND FIGHT

Johansson enjoyed his time as champion, with the paparazzi ready to follow him everywhere, and he was feted everywhere he went, whether in the US, in Sweden, or elsewhere in Europe. After a visit to Egypt, he proposed to his girlfriend before starting training for the rematch.

Patterson, though, had redoubled his efforts to get into shape for the second fight, determined to regain his crown, with the pair eventually meeting in the Polo Grounds in New York in June 1960.

This time it was Johansson who was the favourite for the fight, although following tactics agreed with D'Amato, Patterson was the early aggressor.

All his plans threatened to go awry in the second round when Johansson caught him with another huge right, but this time, he managed to stay on his feet and kept out of trouble for the rest of the round.

Growing increasingly confident that he could handle Johansson's biggest shots, the American seized control, and caught the Swede on the jaw in the fifth round and hurt him. Having missed with a swinging left hook, Patterson caught his opponent and knocked him down.

Johansson got up, but he had a cut above the left eye and was bleeding from the mouth, and the end came soon afterwards. Patterson put him down with another left hook – by his own admission, the hardest punch he ever threw in his career- and knocked the Swede out, his head hitting the canvas, which was audible to those sitting ringside.

Patterson had become the first heavyweight to regain his crown and restore American honour.

Ring Magazine later judged it The Fight of the Year.

THE THIRD FIGHT

What was ultimately the decider between the two men, took place at the Convention Center in Florida in February 1961.

In training for the fight, Johansson had used various sparring partners, including a young Cassius Clay, a future heavyweight champion himself.

This time Patterson was the favourite for the fight with the bookmakers, coming in 12 pounds lighter, which started in explosive fashion.

Both men came out jabbing, but it was Johansson who drew first blood, catching Patterson square on the chin with a right cross that put him down for a count of three. The referee continued counting until eight, a mandatory precaution recently introduced and which both fighters had agreed to adopt.

The Swede looked to press home his advantage, and a swift combination put Patterson down for a second time. Patterson took another mandatory count, but Johansson sensed his moment had come and went for the kill. The champion, though, found some inner resolve through a right and left of his own and knocked down Johansson in turn. It was the first time in more than 40 years that both contenders for the heavyweight crown had been knocked over in the first round, and it was later judged 'Round of the Year."

The intensity did not let up in the next two rounds, with both men catching the other with vicious blows, although they managed to stay on their feet.

A cut appeared above Johansson's left eye in the fourth round, which Patterson saw to exploit, although, in doing so, he had to absorb some heavy blows of his own.

By round five, with Johansson starting to breathe hard, the relentless pace dropped, and Patterson began to assume control.

The end came in the following round after the pair had again exchanged several blows that might have knocked over lesser men. Patterson caught his opponent with a left hook on the forehead and followed that up with two rights that sent the Swede crashing to the canvas. He could not get up in time this time, and he was counted out.

THE AFTERMATH

Patterson had several defences after fighting Johansson in Miami. Still, D'Amato did not allow him to fight the number one contender, Sonny Liston, because he did not want his man fighting anybody with links to organised crime.

However, after a dispute about money, he fired D'Amato and agreed to fight Liston.

It proved an ill-advised move as he lost his heavyweight title to Liston by first-round knock-out in Chicago in 1962. The pair met again the following year, but again Liston knocked him out in the first round.

Following those defeats, Patterson went through a period of depression but recovered and resumed his career.

By 1965 he was the number one contender for the heavyweight title then held by Muhammad Ali (although, much to Ali's disgust, Patterson insisted on calling him Cassius Clay). Patterson's attempt to become a three-time heavyweight champion ended in failure and the fight was stopped in the 12th round.

He would continue fighting until age 37, with his last bout being a rematch with Ali for the NABF heavyweight title, which was stopped in the seventh round with Patterson suffering from a cut eye.

He never fought again, although he never officially announced his retirement.

Later the same year as his final fight with Patterson, Johansson was offered US $100,000 by Clay's promoter to fight the up-and-coming contender. Johansson turned down the opportunity saying, "*That guy couldn't even draw a non-paying crowd, much less any real money.*"

Instead, he returned to Europe, where he captured the European heavyweight crown.

He then fought the British boxer Jack London in a non-title fight, and although he won nearly all the rounds, he seldom threw one of his fearsome right hands.

With just four seconds of the fight remaining, London hit him with a powerful right hand that knocked him flat on his back. He rose at the count of four as the fight ended and was adjudged the winner, but was still groggy afterwards.

The next day when his photos appeared in Stockholm newspapers looking dazed at the final bell, along with the caption "*Wake Up Ingo – you won*', he decided that he had had enough. He wrote to the European Boxing Union, relinquishing his title, and retired at 30.

LATER LIFE

For part of his career, Patterson went into training and trained his adopted son Tracy Harris Patterson, who became the world welterweight champion. They became the first father and son to win world titles in boxing history. He would also train Canadian heavyweight Donovan 'Razor' Ruddock.

His final years were dogged by ill health. He suffered from Alzheimer's (some commentators believe this was brought on by the blows he took in the ring) and prostate cancer, and he died in 2006 at the age of 71.

Patterson was inducted into the International Boxing Hall of Fame in 1991. He said of his career, "*They said that I was the fighter who got knocked down the most, but I also got up the most.*"

Johansson appeared in several movies, and unlike many boxers, he had a successful business career, with interests that included boxing promotion and hotel and bar ownership. He also had a sports apparel line and a range of beer marketed in Sweden under the logo "Hammer" in tribute to his punching power.

He was voted Sweden's third greatest athlete of the 20th century, and, in 2002, he too was inducted into the International Boxing Hall of Fame.

Unfortunately, he, too, contracted Alzheimer's and died in 2009, aged 76.

THE LEGACY

The fights between Patterson and Johansson have sometimes been described as a forgotten rivalry because they happened just before the era of Ali, which has tended to overshadow what came before it in boxing history.

However, the fact that Johansson was able to beat Patterson in that first fight was a hugely significant moment for European boxing, and it would be another 33 years before another European was to hold a recognised version of the heavyweight title.

INTERESTING QUOTES

"Johansson – the hardest I've ever been hit. I don't remember going down or getting up."

- Patterson on Johansson

"Shaking hands with Patterson was like shaking hands with a lace curtain."

- Johansson on Patterson

EMILE GRIFFITH V BENNY PARET

Griffith v Kid

Name	Emile Alphonse Griffith	Bernardo Paret
Height	5 feet (124 cm)	5 feet (124 cm)
Weight	Welterweight, light middleweight, middleweight	Welterweight
Hometown	Saint Thomas, US Virgin Islands	Santa Clara, Cuba
Nickname(s)	N/A	Kid
Overall Career Record	112 fights – 85 wins, 24 losses, 2 draws	50 fights – 35 wins, 12 losses, 3 draws
Head to head	3 fights – 3 wins	3 fights – 3 losses
Style	Orthodox	Orthodox
Recognition	WBA, WBC, NYSAC, and The Ring midweight and welterweight champion	NBA, NYSAC and The Ring welterweight champion

While rivalries between boxers can occasionally escalate to personal and acrimonious levels, few instances have resulted in such a heart-wrenching tragedy as the one that unfolded following the third bout between Emile Griffith and Benny Paret.

It left one man dead and the other with a lifetime of guilt, branded in the eyes of many a murderer.

The accomplishments they had achieved in their careers paled in comparison, serving as a stark reminder, if any reminder was needed, that boxing is a merciless sport where the boundaries between triumph and not just failure but a fate far more grievous are alarmingly fragile.

EMILE GRIFFITH

Griffith was born in the US Virgin Islands in 1938 but moved to the USA as a teenager, following his mother, who had made the same journey a year earlier. A high school dropout with a fine singing voice, he began working in a hat factory in New York.

One day he asked if he could work topless, and the owner, Howie Albert, himself a former amateur boxer, allowed him. He noted his physique and took him to the gym run by famous trainer Gil Clancy.

Later, Clancy said of their collaboration, "*It was the only partnership in history where the Irishman and Jew teamed up, and the mick had the brains.*"

He began boxing as an amateur welterweight, but after winning several Golden Gloves titles, he decided to turn professional.

He lost twice in his first 24 bouts as a professional, fighting often in the New York City area. He moved up the ranks quickly and was soon ready for his first title fight with Paret, his opponent.

However, early in his career, he showed reluctance for his chosen profession and Clancy "really had to instil the killer instinct in him."

BENNY PARET

Benny "The Kid" Paret was born in Cuba in 1937, but the family emigrated to the United States before the revolution, which brought Fidel Castro to power.

In the US, he came under the wing of Manuel Alvaro, who managed him and exercised undue influence on his career.
He made his professional debut in 1954, defeating Oscar Campos in six rounds, and went on to win 12 consecutive fights, six of which were via stoppages.

In 1960, he had his first world title fight against Don Jordan, with the NBA welterweight belt on the line. After 15 rounds, he was awarded the fight by unanimous decision and became champion.

His first defence of the title was against Griffith.

THE ORIGINS OF THE RIVALRY

The root cause of the rivalry was homophobia, with Griffith being gay at a time when being homosexual in the US was regarded as abnormal and classified as a crime. Although he visited gay bars most weekends, he knew it was impossible for him to come out because that was against the whole premise of being a sporting hero.

He also combined being a professional hat designer with his boxing career, and many boxers on the circuit assumed he was gay.

Before the weigh-in for their third fight, Paret was in an upbeat mood, teasing Griffith for being so light. Whilst Griffith had his back turned,

Paret feigned having sex with him whilst his trainers laughed hysterically. He then said, "*Hey, maricon*" (a homosexual slur term) in a provocative voice, "*I'm gonna get you and your husband.*"

Griffith was furious that his sexuality had been demeaned in such a fashion and vowed to exact revenge.

THE FIRST FIGHT

All this, though, was in the future. They met for the first time at the Convention Center in Miami Beach in April 1961. Paret had enjoyed the better of the fight and seemed on course to defend his title at the start of the 13th round.

They came out working each other to the body until the referee separated them near Paret's corner. That was when the challenger threw a long left hook that caught Paret flush on the jaw, leaving him reeling. Sensing his advantage, Griffith hit him with a right and then another left hook, dropping him to the canvas. The champion lay full length whilst the referee counted him out.

REMATCH

Just six months later, they met again in a rematch, which Paret won on a split decision, although many at the time regarded the verdict as controversial. Griffith handed out severe punishment to the challenger, and some even believed that the fight should be stopped at one stage.

After the fight, Griffith offered a comment that would prove to be eerily prophetic "Benny's *a nice boy. But I would like to kill him. And I will if he'll get back in the ring with me.*"

TRAGEDY IN THE RING

Barely two months later, Paret took on middleweight Gene Fullmer and suffered a terrible beating after being knocked out in the sixth round.

Many considered that he was in no shape to fight Griffith for a third time so soon, but he had ambitions of owning a butcher's shop and needed the money to go towards it. His manager also urged him to take the fight because he wanted his share of the prize purse.

For all his bravado at the weigh-in, Paret was actually worried before stepping into the ring with Griffith again. He had tried to persuade his wife, Lucy, to come to the fight at Madison Square Garden in New York, but she preferred to stay in Miami with their son. Lucy had also been battling her own fears, having dreamt for weeks beforehand that her husband would get badly injured.

On the eve of the fight, Benny Paret phoned Lucy and told her that his head hurt and he did not want to fight. She tried to persuade him to withdraw, but he said his manager Alfonso would not allow it because too much money was at stake.

Broadcast live on national television to an audience of watching millions, it was a savage encounter, which Griffith largely dominated, although the outcome might have been different. In the sixth round, a quick combination sent Griffith tumbling to the canvas, and only the bell saved him.

Griffith's trainer Clancy told his fighter to get inside and keep punching until the referee intervened, instructions he was to obey to the letter.

The 12th out of the scheduled 15 rounds was to have a catastrophic outcome. Griffith was still furious, smarting from the words that Paret had directed at him - *"Nobody never called me no faggot before."*

He hit Paret with two brutal right hands that rocked the champion, and although initially, Paret was able to defend himself, he teetered on the ropes with his hands lowered, all resistance gone.

Griffith pinned him against the ropes with his left hand and repeatedly punched Paret in the head with his right. The referee did not hear attempts by Paret's corner to throw in the towel and allowed the onslaught to continue, with Paret's head now outside the ring.

Nearly 30 unanswered blows rained in from Griffith, who had been transformed into a punching machine, twisting his body to get maximum force into each blow before the referee finally stopped the fight.

However, any cheers there may have been swiftly turned to dismay, as, without fists of Griffith to hold him up, the unconscious body of Paret slid to the canvas, his eyes starting to close, watched by a horrified TV audience.

What made matters worse was that Griffith was asked to watch back the final action and comment on it by the NBC broadcaster, *the first time in TV history that a slow motion replay had been used.*

"*I just kept punching*", Griffith said, "*I just kept punching.*"

Paret was rushed to hospital in a coma, but he never regained consciousness and died ten days later. He had suffered severe brain injuries. Griffith did try to visit him, but the hospital would not admit him.

Paret became the youngest boxing world champion to die in the ring and the first on national television.

THE AFTERMATH

Paret died shortly after his 25th birthday and was survived by his wife, Lucy, who was pregnant at the time with their second child. His mother and brother flew from Cuba for the funeral, which 2,500 mourners attended.

Lucy's eldest son kept waiting for his father to come home, and she kept up the pretence that he had gone back to Cuba until she realised he had found out what had happened from somebody else.

The fight would leave a cloud over the sport for many years. NBC in America halted its broadcast of live fights whilst the governor of New York at the time, Nelson Rockefeller, convened a commission to investigate the bout and the sport more generally. However, no blame was ever attached to Griffith personally.

Alfonso was rebuked for allowing his fighter to enter the ring so soon after his last bout, but calls for boxing to be abolished faded away over time.

Boxing, though, would not be shown on national television in the United States again for over a decade.

Ruby Goldstein, the referee on that fateful night, never took charge of another fight.

Griffith was left traumatised, recalling, "*People spit at me in the street. We stayed in a hotel. Every time there was a knock on the door, I would run into the next room, I was so scared.*"

Years later, arriving in Europe for a fight, he saw a headline in a local newspaper, "*Griffith the Killer Arrives.*"

It also meant that, for years, he was often called on to comment whenever there was a boxing fatality. "*It sells, I'm sorry to say, and I don't like it.*"

He also admitted that he was never the same fighter again.

"*After that fight, I did enough to win. I would use my jab all the time. I never wanted to hurt the other guy. I would have quit, but I didn't know how to do anything other than fight.*"

He featured in 80 more fights after the last Paret fight but only won 12 by knock-out. He retired after 18 years as a professional, finishing with a record of 85 wins, 24 losses, two draws and one no-contest.

Griffith would later meet with Paret's elder son for the making of a documentary called 'Ring of Fire" and was absolved of any blame for what happened in the ring that night.

LATER LIFE

Griffith went to his grave, still haunted by what happened in the ring with Paret that night.

He trained several other boxers post-retirement and had a spell coaching the Danish Olympic team. He also worked as an officer at a Juvenile Detention Facility.

In 1992, he was savagely beaten after leaving a gay bar in New York City and spent four months in hospital.

He had been admitted to the Boxing Hall of Fame two years earlier.

He died at the age of 76 in 2013.

THE LEGACY

One of the legacies of the tragic demise of Paret is that boxing officials were forced to re-evaluate when they should step in to stop a fight. Footage from the fight forms part of training videos to this day.

It provided a stark warning of how quickly a situation in the ring can deteriorate and a reminder of how dangerous the sport of boxing can be.

In the Ring of Fire documentary, Griffith relived the moment again "*I can still feel … I-I-I feel … Oh gosh … I get chills, you know, talkin' about him. Sometimes I still have nightmares … I wake up sometime, and I feel my sweat all over my face, I don't know … Memories come back, and there's nothing you can do about it. Just let it flow.*"

INTERESTING QUOTES

"Benny's a nice boy. But I would like to kill him. And I will, if he'll get back in the ring with me."

- Griffith on Paret

"Hey maricon. I'm gonna get you and your husband."

- Paret on Griffith

ERIK MORALES V MARCO ANTONIO BARRERA

El Terrible v The Baby-Faced Assassin

Name	Eric Isaac Morales Elvira	Marco Antonio Barrera Tapie
Height	5 feet 8 inches (173 cm)	5 feet 6 inches (168 cm)
Weight	Super bantamweight, featherweight, super featherweight, lightweight, light welterweight, welterweight	Super flyweight, super bantamweight, featherweight, super featherweight, lightweight
Hometown	Tijuana, Mexico	Mexico City
Nickname(s)	El Terrible (The Terrible)	Baby Faced Assasin, El Barreta, El Baron
Overall Career Record	61 fights – 52 wins, 9 losses	75 fights – 67 wins, 7 losses, 1 No Contest
Head to head	3 fights – 1 win, 2 losses	3 fights – 2 wins, 1 loss
Style	Orthodox	Orthodox
Recognition	WBA, WBC, The Ring lightwelterweight and featherweight champion, WBC and NBF super bantamweight champion	WBA and WBO lightweight champion, WBC and The Ring featherweight champion, WBO super bantamweight champion

Whilst hostility between fighters can often be manufactured in order to help promote and sell fights, there was nothing artificial about the rivalry between the two Mexicans, Erik Morales and Marco Antonio Barrera.

They genuinely did not like each other and sought to prove it with a trilogy of fights that lives long in the memory. They fought 36 fiercely contested rounds, but there was no mutual congratulation when it was all over. Instead, they refused to shake each other's hands or share an embrace.

It was a sporting rivalry that became intensely personal and divided the country. The two fighters had contrasting styles. Morales was a tall, talented puncher, whilst Barrera, the shorter, stouter man, preferred to get in close. Added to that, the pair came from different backgrounds and parts of the country, and all the ingredients were there to make the competition between the pair fierce and bitter.

Put a world title at stake, and the fuse was lit.

ERIK MORALES

Morales, who became known by the nickname "El Terrible", was born in a working-class district of Tijuana in 1976.

Inspired by his father, who had been a fighter himself, he began boxing at five years old. He went on to have a highly impressive amateur career, winning eleven major titles in Mexico and finishing with 108 wins from his 114 fights.

He turned professional aged 16 and quickly began climbing the super bantamweight division ranks. He was soon ready to challenge for his first world title, fighting Daniel Zaragoza for the WBC belt in September 1997. He knocked him out in eleven rounds to become the champion.

Several successful defences of his title followed before he beat another former champion Junior Jones – who had twice previously beaten Barrera – knocking him out in the fourth round.

Another tough fight against Northern Irishman Wayne McCullough followed before he was ready to step into the ring with Barrera for the first time.

MARCO ANTONIO BARRERA

Barrera was born in 1974, the son of a businessman who wanted him to take over his undertakings. However, he was interested in boxing from an early age, partly due to an older brother who was an amateur boxer himself and had enjoyed some success fighting locally.

As an amateur, Barrera won five Mexican titles before becoming professional when he was 15. Although he knew he wanted a career in boxing, Barrera continued his studies at the same time and went to university to study law. However, he then dropped out to concentrate on his sporting career.

Initially, nicknamed 'The Babyface Assassin', he debuted as a super flyweight before moving up to super bantamweight. He had his first world title fight in 1995, defeating Daniel Jiménez of Puerto Rica on points for the WBO version of the title.

Four successful defences followed before he suffered his first professional career loss to Jones. Barrera was disqualified because his cornerman entered the ring before the referee could stop the fight.

He then lost the rematch unanimously on points.

Barrera then retired from boxing, only to make his comeback a year later, and he regained his WBO belt, beating Richie Wenton.

By 2000, a match was made for him to fight Morales for the first time in their careers.

THE ORIGINS OF THE RIVALRY

Their rivalry was partly due to the fact that they came from different backgrounds and parts of Mexico.

Morales was raised in a working-class ghetto district of Tijuana, whilst Barrera was an educated, middle-class boy raised in a suburb of Mexico City.

Adding to that were rumours of a knockdown during a training session, whilst Barrera later recalled, "*We had many problems and many problems in the press. We had problems playing football, and members of our teams switched sides, and there was a lot of gossip going around between the two camps.*"

In the run-up to their second fight, Morales commented on his rival's sexuality using a Mexican slur. When he repeated it at a press conference featuring the two boxers in Houston, Barrera hit Morales with a right hand, and a brief brawl ensued.

Barrera later said of his rival, "*I think he's an excellent boxer and a marvellous champion. But as a person, he's insular. He doesn't think, talks for talking sake, and he's annoyed me greatly by behaving in this ridiculous way.*"

THE FIRST FIGHT

In February 2000, they met for the first time with the WBA Super Bantamweight title on the line.

From the outset, the action flowed to and fro, although Barrera had the better of the early exchanges, through short, sharp hooks to the body, which Morales tried to counter with his right hand.

The tone for the fight was set in the first round when Morales accidentally caught his opponent with a low blow. When he tried to apologise, Barrera refused to touch gloves. By the end of the fourth round, Barrera was ahead on points, but the round that followed became iconic.

In a bout that was itself named "*Fight of the Year*", the fifth round was called "*Round of the Year*."

Morales was hit by a right hand and, pinned against the ropes, appeared to be in trouble. Still, he hit back in devastating fashion, catching Barrera with an uppercut and raining down a series of unanswered punches on his opponent.

A lesser man would have buckled, but not Barrera, who soon regrouped and began to hit back. By the end of the round, they were slugging it out, blow for blow, sending the crowd into frenzy.

The intensity scarcely let up in the rounds that succeeded until they reached the 12th and last round with Barrera ahead, according to most watchers.

At this point, Barrera decided to change tactics and fought on the back foot, catching Morales with a left hook that left Morales clinging to the ropes. Morales went down, although some argue that it was a push and others that it was a slip. The referee, though, judged it a knockdown and declared the round 10 – 8 in favour of Barrera.

Both men threw their hands in the air in triumph at the end of the fight, but most neutrals expected the fight to be given to Barrera. The judges, though, had other ideas.

One gave it to Barrera by a single point, another to Morales by the same margin, whilst, to the surprise of many, Dalby Shirley gave it 115 – 112 in favour of Morales.

In retrospect, it can be argued that, although Barrera had thrown more punches, Morales had been the more accurate of the two.

What was certain was that there would be a rematch because they had provided so much entertainment, there was an insatiable appetite for them to do it again.

Speaking afterwards, Morales said, "*We were both hurt during the fight. He was the biggest puncher I ever faced in the ring.*" He also said, "*People needed a great fight, and we gave it to them.*"

THE REMATCH

After several successful title defences, Morales moved up a weight, began fighting as a featherweight, and soon became WBC Flyweight Champion.

Barrera had also moved up and soon handed Naseem Hamed, who was considered the lineal Flyweight Champion, his first defeat in the classification.

The scene was set for the two to meet again, this time for the WBC belt.

This time round, Barrera changed his tactics, and instead of slugging it out with his opponent from the opening bell, he was content, at least in the opening rounds, to conserve his energy for later in the fight.

If the first fight had energised the crowd, the lacklustre performance of Barrera, in particular, frustrated them this time.

He did cut his opponent on the bridge of the nose in the second round, but by the halfway stage, Morales appeared clearly ahead.

Barrera did, though, get stronger, although he was put on the canvas in the seventh round, the referee judging it a slip.

In the following round, Morales was cut over his right eye.

However, he seemed to shade rounds 10 and 11, which combined with his dominance in the earlier rounds, in the eyes of many observers, was enough for him to shade the verdict.

Again both men raised their arms in triumph at the final bell, and many at ringside thought Morales had won the fight.

The three judges, though, had a different opinion and gave it to Barrera unanimously.

It was the first defeat of Morales' professional career.

THE THIRD FIGHT

Two years later, the pair met for what would be the final time, this time as Super Featherweights.

Morales had unified both the WBC and IBF titles coming into the fight, whilst Barrera was on the comeback trail, having been defeated by Manny Pacquiao, and was making his debut at the weight.

In contrast to the second fight, it was Barrera who started the stronger, despite giving away both pounds and inches to his opponent. He had Morales in trouble in the first round and bloodied his nose in the second, but Morales came back stronger in the latter half of the fight and won four out of the last six rounds, according to the judges.

The last two rounds, in particular, were memorable because they brought back memories of their first contest, as the two went toe to toe and slugged it out.

In the end, one of the commentators breathlessly summed up, saying, *"They'll savagely trade until the final bell! My God, what a fight! What these two guys have given to the sport can't be quantified."*

The bout was again voted *"Fight of the Year."*

Again it went to the judges, and whilst one had it down as a draw, two others ruled in favour of Barrera, who became the new WBC super featherweight champion. Afterwards, Barrera described it as *"the most rewarding fight of my career."*

THE AFTERMATH

Morales continued to fight and caused a memorable upset by defeating Pacquiao. He moved up to lightweight in a bid to become the first Mexican to win world titles at four different weights but began to struggle, Pacquiao twice getting his revenge.

However, in the twilight of his career, he did achieve his ambition when he beat compatriot Pablo Cesar Cano in Las Vegas.

He retired in 2014, winning 52 of his 61 fights.

Barrera had four defences of his title and added the IBF belt to his collection, but then lost to fellow Mexican Juan Manuel Marquez and in his rematch with Pacquiao. Although he continued fighting, his appearances became less frequent until he decided to retire at the age of 37.

He retired with 67 wins from 74 fights, reflecting, "*I fought whoever I had to fight. I didn't leave anything pending, so I think I left boxing at the right time.*"

LATER LIFE

Morales has spent much of his time since retirement managing a parks and recreation department in Tijuana with a US $3.5 million annual budget, devoting back part of the salary he receives. His justification for doing so is that this is "*Just a way for me to be able to thank the people who have been so good to me all my life.*"

He has also pursued a political career, winning a seat in the Mexican Congress and currently serves in the legislative body's committee on sports.

Barrera pursued a successful career as a boxing commentator and is involved in the media.

THE LEGACY

At the time, this was one of the most bitter and personal rivalries in boxing, and the three fights between the two are regarded as classics.

Improbably, as time has passed, the hatred has been replaced by friendship, and when Morales was inducted into the Nevada Boxing Hall of Fame in 2017, Barrera sponsored him.

Today, they even collaborate on a successful podcast together.

Morales said, "*When we were young, we did what we had to do*", and "*Things happen, but we are friends. Time heals all wounds.*"

Interesting Quotes

"He was the biggest puncher I ever faced in the ring."
- Morales on Barrera

"I think he's an excellent boxer and a marvellous champion. But as a person he's insular, he doesn't think, talks for talking sake, and he's annoyed me greatly by behaving in this ridiculous way."
- Barrera on Morales

MUHAMMAD ALI V KEN NORTON

The People's Champion v The Jaw Breaker

Name	Cassius Marcellus Clay Jr. (later changed his name to Muhammad Ali)	Kenneth Howard Norton Sr.
Height	6 foot 3 inches (191 cm)	6 foot 3 inches (191 cm)
Weight	Light heavyweight, heavyweight	Heavyweight
Hometown	Louisville, Kentucky	Jackson, Illinois
Nickname(s)	The Louisville Lip, The Greatest, The People's Champion	The Black Hercules. The Jawbreaker, The Fighting Marine
Overall Career Record	61 fights – 56 wins, 5 losses	50 fights – 42 wins, 7 losses, 1 draw
Head to head	3 fights - 2 wins, 1 loss,	3 fights – 1 win, 2 losses
Style	Orthodox	Orthodox
Recognition	WBA, WBC, The Ring, NABF and NYSAC heavyweight champion, Olympic gold medallist	WBA, NABF heavyweight champion

The history books will show Muhammad Ali winning three fights against Ken Norton 2-1. The reality, though, was somewhat different. Ali only won the second bout on a split decision, and, whilst all three judges awarded him the third, many observers at ringside argue that was a travesty of justice and that the verdict should have gone the other way.

Even some contemporary commentators have found it hard to make a case for Ali winning that decision.

Indeed, after the perceived injustice of that decision, Norton - by his admission never quite had the same motivation again when he stepped in the ring. Ali ensured there would never be a fourth fight, saying Norton was too difficult an opponent.

MUHAMMAD ALI

The story of Muhammad Ali is well-known. Born Cassius Clay in Louisville, Kentucky (hence the nickname 'The Louisville Lip'), he began boxing at 12. He enjoyed a highly successful amateur career, winning gold in the light heavyweight class at the Rome Olympics in 1960.
He turned professional soon afterwards, moving up a weight and beginning a long association with the trainer Angelo Dundee.

Eventually, he earned a title shot in 1964 against Sonny Liston, a man regarded as virtually unbeatable at the time.

During that fight, he taunted the champion setting the tone for much of his career to follow, then knocking him out.

After converting to Islam, Clay changed his name to Muhammad Ali, and for the next three years, he was the undisputed heavyweight champion.

In 1967, though, he was stripped of his title and had his boxing licence suspended because he refused to be drafted into the US Army and to fight in Vietnam, saying, "*I ain't got no quarrel with those Vietcong.*"

Whilst he was out of the ring, a number of new heavyweight contenders had emerged, including Joe Frazier, who would eventually succeed him as champion.

After his suspension was rescinded, he would fight Frazier in the first of a brutal trilogy, losing narrowly.

It was Ali's first professional loss.

He was still rebuilding his reputation before he agreed to fight Norton for the first time in March 1973.

KEN NORTON

Born in Jacksonville, Illinois, Norton was an outstanding athlete in high school, playing in defence in an all-star (American) football team and winning seven out of eight events he entered in high school athletics meetings. As a result, Illinois introduced the 'Ken Norton' rule restricting athletes in high school meets in the State to a maximum of four events.

He went to college on a football scholarship and then, after leaving school, enlisted in the US Marines. While he was with the military, he began boxing and soon became an outstanding heavyweight.

He turned professional and began to work his way through the ranks, ascribing his progress to the motivational book '*Think and Grow Rich*' by Napoleon Hill, which he said "*changed my life dramatically. I was a green fighter, yet I won, all through reading this book.*"

THE ORIGINS OF THE RIVALRY

Although Ali would dismiss Norton as an amateur before their first fight, this was just his normal disparagement of a rival, and there were no overtones of anything darker, unlike, for example, his rivalry with Frazier.

However, there was no doubt that Norton's style caused him problems. He used an unorthodox crab-like defence, in which he would cross his arms, with his left arm positioned across his torso and his other up by one of his ears. That left little room for his opponent to extend their arms, and he would attack from a crouch position, firing well-placed punches into the body and face of the man he was fighting against.

After Norton passed away, Gene Kilroy, who knew both men well, said, *"He had that awkward style, where he'd shoot his jab up from the waist, and it was very unusual. Most guys throw the jab from the shoulder, and that always gave Ali trouble."*

THE FIRST FIGHT (THE 'JAW BREAKER')

Ali was supremely confident going into the fight, regarding it as no more than a tune-up for bigger and better things to come. The 5 – 1 favourite with the bookmakers, he entered the ring wearing a white robe encrusted with jewels and rhinestones, with the words 'People's Choice' emblazoned on the back, a gift from music superstar Elvis Presley.

However, from the outset, it was clear that this would be no walkover, with Ali struggling to cope with Norton's style. And it was Norton who caused the early damage, throwing his left hook to devastating effect and, according to Ali and Dundee, breaking his jaw in the second round. Ali would later say, *"Imagine you have your jaw broken and have to fight ten more rounds."*

Norton would later dispute this version of events, insisting that he did not break Ali's jaw until the final 12th round, but what was not in doubt was the outcome. Norton had won by split decision.

In his autobiography later, Norton said about the fight, *"Life's battles don't always go to the stronger or faster man, but sooner or later, the man who wins is the man who thinks he can."*

It was only Ali's second defeat of his career.

THE REMATCH

The rematch came six months later in Inglewood, California. Norton entered the ring five pounds lighter than he had in the first fight with Ali, leaving some to wonder if he had over-trained.

Ali, meanwhile, was determined to get his revenge.

With his jaw recovered, he had absented himself from his usual celebrity lifestyle. Instead, he had endured a monastic existence in training camp, where he would run for hours and endure painful rub-downs.

It meant that when Ali stepped into the ring in California, the crowd saw a slicker, leaner version of the fighter.

The renewed dedication seemed to pay off in the early rounds, with Ali controlling the fight and refusing to sit down at the bell, instead continuing to dance whilst listening to instructions from Dundee.

However, with few of his punches lacking any real impact, Norton kept pressing forward. He caught Ali with several big shots, yelling out triumphantly, "*I own you,*" as Ali headed back to his corner at the end of the fifth round.

From there, the two went head to toe, Ali trying to out-box his opponent, but at the cost of taking some heavy blows from Norton, who would not back down.

By the time it came to the final round, Norton was clearly the stronger man and the outcome of the fight was in the balance. Perhaps sensing this, Ali came out rejuvenated, catching his opponent with a series of combination shots.

It was enough for him to win the round and, with it, the fight. But only just. One judge gave the fight to Norton, the other two to Ali, whilst, in a poll of ringside journalists, Ali just edged it.

In the post-fight interviews, Ali acknowledged his struggles saying, "*I'm in good condition, but I'm tireder than usual…because of my age.*" He added: "*If I wasn't in this shape, no way I could've won.*"

And he also praised Norton, describing him as the "*next best in the world after myself.*"

THE DECIDER

By the time they met for a third and what would be the final time, Ali had become heavyweight champion again, regaining his title in sensational fashion by knocking-out George Foreman in their fight in Zaire that became known as 'The Rumble in the Jungle'. Despite his victory, many observers believed that this marked the decline of Ali as a fighter, with his once lightening quick reflexes now blunted.

By the time he stepped back into the ring with Norton, he had also survived the 'Thriller in Manila' - the third fight in his trilogy with Frazier, in which, by his own admission, Ali had come as close to death as he ever came in his boxing career.

Norton had fought Foreman for the heavyweight title but was knocked out in the second round. Despite that loss, he had maintained his place among the leading contenders of the time and was the younger man by nearly two years.

Going into the fight, the narrative was that Ali was no longer the same physical specimen and that if he were made to go the full distance, he would struggle. There was also a suggestion that if it went to the judges, then almost inevitably, the result would go in his favour.

Indeed, one version of the story is that Norton was robbed, with the ringside commentator proclaiming he would be "*very surprised*" if Norton had not won the fight.

Boxing Monthly once described the decision as the fifth most controversial in the history of the sport, whilst latter-day boxing writers have struggled to justify the judges scoring.

However, just like the other two bouts, it was a very close fight, with Ali struggling to cope with Norton's style but still managing to land the occasional blow.

The statistics back up Norton's case. Whilst Ali threw more punches, 709, only 199 landed, whereas Norton was successful with 286 of the 635 punches he produced. Norton also produced more power punches – 192 as opposed to 128.

For all that, though, Norton's corner may have made a mistake, telling their man that the result was in the bag at the end of the penultimate round. Ali came out for the 15th round determined to mount one final effort, which may have tipped the balance in his favour.

Ali was awarded the fight on both the judges' and referee's scorecards. However, the margin was razor thin, with one judge giving seven rounds to Norton and another six, with a further round drawn.

Norton was very upset after the fight saying, "*I won at least nine or ten rounds. I was robbed*", whilst Ali, for once, was more restrained after his victory "*I honestly thought he beat me in Yankee Stadium, but the judges gave it to me, and I'm grateful to them.*"

He also closed down any talk of another fight with Norton. "*Kenny's style is too difficult for me. I can't beat him, and I sure don't want to fight him again.*"

THE AFTERMATH

Ali announced he was retiring from boxing after the third fight with Norton to concentrate on his faith, but he soon returned, although he was no longer the fighter he had been in his prime.

He lost his title to the virtually unknown Leon Spinks in 1978, only to get it back in a rematch, becoming the first man to win the heavyweight championship three times.

Then he retired again, beginning to suffer from the vocal stutters and trembling hands that signaled the onset of his Parkinson's disease. An ill-advised comeback against Larry Holmes was stopped after the fourth round when Angelo Dundee threw the towel in to prevent his man from suffering any more punishment.

Norton briefly held a version of the world championship when his victory over Jimmy Young was given title status when Spinks chose to fight Ali again rather than him.

In the first defence of his WBC title, he lost his title by a very close decision to Larry Holmes, who would go on to become the third-longest reigning heavyweight champion in history.

He would have several more bouts before deciding to retire from the sport at the age of 37.

He would come back and have another title shot when he fought Gerry Cooney, but the fight was stopped in the first round.

LATER LIFE

Although Ali was to remain a major personality for the rest of his life, his health was in decline.

When he died in 2016 at 74, his passing was mourned by millions worldwide, and his memorial service was watched by an estimated 1 billion people worldwide. The pallbearers at his funeral would include Larry Holmes, George Foreman, Lennox Lewis and Mike Tyson.

He was buried in Louisville, and the city's mayor declared, "*Muhammad Ali belongs to the world. But he only has one hometown.*"

Whilst he was still boxing, Norton would appear in a major Hollywood movie, Mandingo, playing the part of a pre-Civil War slave. He would appear in the sequel and had bit parts in several other films.

He also worked as a boxing commentator and started a sports management company, representing athletes in contract negotiations.

In 1986 he was involved in a near-fatal car accident that left him with slurred speech.

He also published his autobiography and appeared in a documentary with Ali, Foreman, Frazier, and Holmes called 'Champions Forever', discussing their various careers.

Inducted into the World Boxing Hall of Fame in 1999, he died in 2013 at 70.

THE LEGACY

Whilst the trilogy of fights that Ali fought with Frazier is better known, few boxers posed a more significant challenge to the champion than Norton with his unconventional style.

Perhaps Norton would be even better remembered had either the verdict in the second or third fights gone his way, but he can certainly look back on his career with a great deal of satisfaction, and he played his part in creating the legend that is Ali.

INTERESTING QUOTES

"Kenny's style is too difficult for me. I can't beat him, and I sure don't want to fight him again."

- Ali on Norton

"They called us all handsome. Muhammad they called pretty. But The fairest of them all Ken Norton."

- George Foreman on Norton

"He's an exceptional athlete who has tremendous pride. He has the ability to give more than 100 percent. He reached back against me when there wasn't much left, in our second fight, and won the final round, which saved the fight for him on two of the official cards. He also reached back in Manila against Joe Frazier when it seemed the fight was lost. The great ones have this ability, so I would definitely call Ali a great fighter."

- Norton on Ali

SUGAR RAY LEONARD V THOMAS HEARNS

Sugar Ray v The Hitman

Name	Ray Charles Leonard	Thomas Hearns
Height	5 feet two inches (186 cm)	6 feet one inch (185 cm)
Weight	Welterweight, light middleweight, middleweight, super middleweight, light heavyweight	Welterweight, light middleweight, middleweight, super middleweight, light heavyweight, cruiserweight
Hometown	Wilmington, North Carolina	Grand Junction, Tennessee
Nickname(s)	Sugar Ray	The Hitman, Motor City Cobra
Overall Career Record	40 fights – 36 wins, 3 losses, 1 defeat	67 fights – 61 wins, 5 losses, 1 draw
Head to head	2 fights – 1 win, 1 draw	2 fights– 1 loss, 1 draw
Style	Orthodox	Orthodox
Recognition	WBC and The Ring welterweight champion, WBC super-middleweight champion, WBC light heavyweight champion Olympic gold medalist	First man in history to win world titles in five different weight categories – welterweight, light middleweight, middleweight, super middleweight, light heavyweight

For some boxing fans, the era of 'The Four Kings' in the 1980s was a special one. Not only were Sugar Ray Leonard, Thomas Hearns, Roberto Duran and Marvin Hagler all great fighters and distinct personalities in their own right, but they fought against each other.

Between them, they fought nine world championship fights over the course of a decade, helping the sport of boxing revive in the eyes of the public following the fallow period post the retirement of Muhammad Ali.

Those fights include four knock-outs, whilst three were voted fights of the year.

Even among these, the first fight between Leonard and Hearns would stand out both as a symbol of the age and as a microcosm of the greater rivalries between all four.

SUGAR RAY LEONARD

Ray Charles Leonard was born in North Carolina in 1956, although the family subsequently migrated, first to Washington and then Maryland.

It was his older brother Roger who first encouraged him to get into boxing. Roger had joined a local club and won some trophies, something that Leonard wanted to emulate. He soon acquired the nickname, Sugar Ray – after boxing great Sugar Ray Robinson – and it would not be long before he was out-stripping anything that his brother had done in the ring, enjoying great success in the amateur ranks.

The culmination of his amateur career was when he was picked to represent the US at the 1976 Olympics in Montreal, Canada, boxing in the welterweight division.

He won all six of his bouts in Montreal, winning the final by a unanimous points decision, and chose that moment to retire from the sport, insisting that it was time for him to go back to school.

The reality, though, intervened when he discovered that his girlfriend at the time was pregnant and that she intended to sue him for child support.

With both his parents ill at the same time and without any other obvious means of making money, Leonard was forced to re-evaluate his options and decided that, after all, he would begin a professional career in boxing.

He made rapid headway in the sport, especially after teaming up with Angelo Dundee – Muhammad Ali's former trainer and manager – and he won his first 25 fights, 16 of them via knock-out.

He won the WBC Welterweight title in 1979, beating Wilfred Benítez at Caesar's Palace in 1979, and, after a successful defence against the British challenger Dave 'Boy' Green, he met one of the other Four Kings, Roberto Durán, for the first time.

Durán won the first fight, nicknamed *'The Brawl in Montreal'*, on points, but Leonard got his revenge in New Orleans five months later when Durán quit in the eighth round uttering the words "*No Más*" (no more).

The following year he agreed to fight Hearns in a welterweight unification contest.

TOMMY HEARNS

Thomas Hearns was born in Tennessee in 1958 and was raised by his mother, along with eight other siblings. When he was five years old, the family moved to Detroit, which was to give him one of his later nicknames, *'The Motor City Cobra'*, although he was more famously known as "The Hitman."

After taking up boxing, he had a highly successful amateur career, finishing with a record of 155 wins from 163 fights and winning championships at light welterweight.

In 1977 he turned professional under the tutelage of trainer Emanuel Steward, who is credited with changing his boxing style. Known as a comparatively light puncher in his amateur days, it was Stewart who discovered the potential in his right hand, transforming him into one of the biggest hitters of his era.

Hearns would knock out his first 17 professional opponents and, having won all of his first 28 fights, was ready for his first world title shot against Mexico's Pipino Cuevas, who had held the WBA welterweight championship for four years. Hearns beat him by Technical Knock-Out in the second round.

He was named Fighter of the Year in 1980.

THE ORIGINS OF THE RIVALRY

The contest between the two was viewed as a battle between a boxer and a puncher. Leonard exemplified the former. He had fast hands and feet, and an even quicker brain, with the ability to out-think more physically intimidating opponents. Hearns was far more of a puncher, with an explosive right hand capable of doing immense damage in a matter of seconds.

They also had contrasting personalities. Leonard was an extrovert and used his celebrity status to earn millions in product endorsements, selling anything from cars to soda. Hearns was more low-key, spoke softly, and exuded an air of menace. He was also more blue-collar than Leonard, having been brought up in poor neighbourhoods in Detroit.

Yet Hearns always seemed to be surrounded by an ever-growing circle of friends and admirers, with Stewart saying he had the biggest entourage of anybody in boxing.

But there was nothing personal about the rivalry. In later years, Hearns would say, "*We're good friends. We made each other a lot of money, so we've been friends for a while now.*"

THE FIRST FIGHT ("THE SHOWDOWN")

Few bouts have been as widely anticipated as the first fight between the two, which was billed as 'The Showdown." At one stage, though, it looked like it might have to be postponed after Leonard suffered an eye injury whilst sparring in training for the fight.

He downplayed the incident, insisting there would be no postponement, although, when word leaked out about what had happened, the betting odds, which had made him favourite, began to shift in favour of Hearns.

When they finally climbed into the ring together at Caesar's Palace, it was not only to a sell-out crowd in the arena, but it was shown live on closed circuit TV in nearly 300 locations in the US and Canada. And some 50 countries either broadcast the fight live or showed highlights.

The first five rounds were cagey, each man attempting to sound the other out with feints and jabs, although the consensus was that Hearns had the better of them.

In the sixth round, though, Leonard made his move, catching Hearns on the jaw with a stiff left that caused his knees to buckle. Leonard followed that up with hooks to the body and continued the assault into the seventh round, catching his opponent frequently and sending him reeling across the ring.

It was Steward in Hearns' corner who came to the rescue of his fighter, urging him to change his style. "*You've got to be the boxer now. Get on the bicycle. Stick and move.*"

Hearns took him at his word, and, for the next three rounds, the roles were reversed, with Hearns now the one dancing around the ring, whilst it was Leonard who was now the one looking for the one big punch to end it all.

It was Hearns who now took control of the fight, catching Leonard repeatedly, who was beginning to suffer from a badly swollen left eye.

It was the turn of Dundee in Leonard's corner to make a fateful intervention. As his fighter trudged wearily back to his corner at the end of the 12th round, he told him, "*You're blowing it now, son, you're blowing it.*

We need fire, and you're not firing! You're blowing it, Ray. You've got to be quicker! You've got to take it away from him! Speed!"

His words galvanised Leonard, who at that point was trailing on the scorecards of all three judges, into action, and he came storming out for the start of the 13th round. He caught Hearns with a right, which made his knees buckle again, and then rained in punches, landing 25 unanswered blows that left Hearns dazed and confused and hanging over the ropes.

Hearns, somehow, made it through to the end of the round and even came out for the next, but he had nothing left to give by that stage. The referee Davey Pearl stopped the fight, later saying, "*When I didn't hear anybody shouting at me from Hearns' corner, I realised I had done the right thing.*"

Years later, watching back the fight and asked what he would have done differently, Hearns said, "*I probably would have done more punching than I did. Also, I would have given him more angles. I'd have given him different angles after every attack.*"

However, he was not too critical of his younger self, "*I do look upon it as a good performance from myself. I fought hard, we both did, and I put on a great show.*"

Ring Magazine named it Fight of the Year for 1981, and it is regularly included in lists of the greatest fights of all time.

THE REMATCH

Despite immediate calls for a rematch, it would actually be eight years before they fought again, in part because Leonard decided to retire after discovering he had a detached retina whilst training, using the opportunity of a charity event to announce that he did not want to box any more.

Several comebacks followed, and, during the course of one of them, he earned a controversial split decision over another of the Four Kings, Marvin Hagler.

By this time, he had moved up to super middleweight, and promoters were finally able to agree on another fight with Hearns.

Meanwhile, Hearns had also moved up the weight divisions, first becoming the undisputed Light Middleweight champion and then venturing up a division to challenge Hagler for the middleweight title. He lost but garnered a great deal of respect from boxing fans for how he fought and the courage he showed.

He would win further titles at three different weight divisions before he climbed into the ring with Leonard again.

Their fight was again scheduled for Caesar's Palace, with the pair agreeing to fight at a catch-weight limit of 164 pounds each, rather than the normal super middleweight limit of 168 pounds, although both came in below the revised limit anyway.

On the morning of the fight came the news that Hearns' younger brother had been arrested for shooting his girlfriend, but when he learned of the incident, Hearns refused to be distracted, saying, "*This is not going to affect me. Look, I'm here to do a job--I've been waiting eight years to knock this guy out.*"

It was another very close contest with little to tell them apart, but it was Hearns who scored the two knockdowns, dropping Leonard in the third round and again in round 11 after striking him with consecutive rights.

Leonard, though, had a big fifth round and claimed the final round, and in the end, that was enough to earn him a draw, much to the dissatisfaction of many at ringside and watching on television, who thought Hearns had done enough to have won it.

Both fighters, though, accepted the decision. Leonard reflected that "*I think we've both showed we're champions*", whilst Hearns said, "*I respect their decision. I'm proud I had a draw. The judges could have ruled that I lost. So I'm thankful for what I have.*"

Again reflecting later, Hearns said, "*I was a better fighter in '89. I worked harder. I trained harder.*"

Leonard has since admitted that Hearns should have got the decision.

THE AFTERMATH

Leonard would go on to meet Durán for a third time, although it proved to be an anti-climax as he won easily. However, his career ended on a down note with successive defeats to Terry Norris and, after another period spent in retirement, Hector Camacho.

Hearns would enjoy one more big day in the sun when he beat Virgil Hill to win the WBA light heavyweight title to his collection.
He would not finally retire until 2006, although he was way past his best by then.

LATER LIFE

For many years Leonard worked as a boxing analyst but has also appeared in numerous television shows and several movies and remains a celebrity figure in the US.

He has made a fortune from advertising deals and is now a highly sought-after motivational speaker, both in the United States and overseas.

In addition, he is heavily involved in charitable work, with the issue of juvenile diabetes a particular cause for which he campaigns.

Hearns initially seemed to have managed the money he made from boxing wiser than most, but years of extravagant spending coupled with some unwise investments saw him squander his fortune, and he was forced to auction off his possessions to pay his debts.

He enjoyed a later career as a professional wrestler and has collaborated with some of his former protagonists on boxing documentaries looking back at the era of the Four Kings.

Both men have been inducted into the Boxing Hall of Fame.

THE LEGACY

Arguably no single fight epitomised the "Four Kings" more than the first one between Leonard and Hearns, with the two men going toe to toe, slugging it out until the end. The fact that the result could have gone either way is a testament to the skill and courage of both men.

No quarter was asked or given.

INTERESTING QUOTES

"I think we've both showed we're champions."

- Sugar Ray Leonard on Hearns

"On hearing his brother had been arrested for murder on the eve of their second fight "This is not going to affect me. Look, I'm here to do a job--I've been waiting eight years to knock this guy out"

- Hearns on Sugar Ray Leonard

CHRIS EUBANK V NIGEL BENN

Simply the Best v The Dark Destroyer

Name	Christopher Livingston Eubank	Nigel Gregory Benn
Height	5 feet 10 inches (178 cm)	5 feet 9.5 inches (177 cm)
Weight	Middleweight, super middleweight, cruiserweight	Middleweight, super middleweight
Hometown	Dulwich, London	Ilford, East London
Nickname(s)	Simply the Best, English	The Dark Destroyer
Overall Career Record	52 fights – 45 wins, 5 losses, 2 draws	48 fights – 42 wins, 5 losses, 1 draw
Head to head	2 fights – 1 win, 1 draw	2 fights – 1 loss, 1 draw
Style	Orthodox	Orthodox
Recognition	WBO super middleweight champion, WBO middleweight champion, WBC middleweight champion	WBC super-middleweight champion, WBO super middleweight champion, Commonwealth middleweight champion

There was a period in the early 1990s when the middleweight division of boxing was dominated by British fighters, with bouts between them drawing TV audiences across the world running into the hundreds of millions.

Unfortunately, and as a reminder of what a brutal sport boxing can be, several of these fights had tragic consequences for some of those involved.

In particular, there was real antipathy between two fighters, Chris Eubank and Nigel Benn, which continues to this day. Both have sons that went on to box and were due to fight each other before more controversy got in the way.

CHRIS EUBANK

Chris Eubank was born in South London in 1966 but spent part of his early childhood in Jamaica. He returned to London, where he lived in impoverished circumstances and frequently found himself in trouble at school, once being expelled 18 times in a year.

At the age of 16, his father sent him to New York to live with his mother, and it was there that he began training regularly at the Jerome Boxing Club, following in the footsteps of his twin elder brothers.

He would later claim in his autobiography that bullying from his brothers made him want to succeed and be accepted as an individual in his own right.

As an amateur, Eubank featured in Golden Gloves events before turning professional at the age of 19.

Although he won his early fights, he went largely unnoticed until he fought on the undercard of a Nigel Benn fight, who was a rising star. The fact that he beat Jamaican Anthony Logan, who had almost beaten Benn himself in an earlier fight, indicated that Eubank was a man who should be taken seriously.

Returning to England, Eubank decided to base himself in Brighton and set his sights on Benn, believing he could beat him.

Following a series of victories by stoppage, Eubank captured the WBC International title in 1990 and, later that same year, knocked out Reinaldo dos Santos in 20 seconds, including the count. With the demand from British boxing fans growing louder, it was time for him to fight Benn for the first time.

NIGEL BENN

Benn was born in East London in 1964. He joined the British Army at the age of 18, where he spent three years in West Germany before moving to Northern Ireland.

Apocryphally, his first competitive fight happened outside a nightclub in Yorkshire when a local bare-knuckle champion, Karl "The Equaliser" Smith, asked him to step outside, threatening to beat Benn into submission. Smith had much the worst of the encounter.

Benn turned professional in 1987 and won his first 22 fights by knock-out, most of them within the opening two or three rounds.

In the course of that run, he claimed the vacant Commonwealth Middleweight title beating Abdul Umaru in two rounds.

However, he lost his title the following year to another British fighter, Michael Watson, in a fight that was even broadcast on national television in the US. Benn was the heavy favourite going into the fight, but relying almost exclusively on hooks, struggled to penetrate Watson's defences and gradually exhausted himself. Then, in the sixth round, Watson caught him with a shot that put him down, and he failed to beat the count.

He resurrected his career in the United States, eventually earning the right to fight Doug DeWitt for the WBO Middleweight title. DeWitt put him down in the second round, but Benn responded with a knockdown of his own in the next round and then claimed the title by sending the champion to the canvas three times in the eighth round.

Having beaten Iran Barkley in his first defence, he returned to the UK to fight Eubank.

The Origins of the Rivalry

The two were a study in contrasts. Benn had earned himself the nickname "The Dark Destroyer", not only for how he beat most of his opponents so easily but also for the air of brooding menace he exuded. However, Eubank was a showman. He cultivated his reputation for extravagant behaviour, both in and out of the ring, would win awards for his dress sense, and read PG Wodehouse to improve himself.

He would later express the difference between him and Benn as being "*like two minds which are miles apart, a street brain and a society brain.*"

Eubank considered himself socially and intellectually better than Benn, something which greatly irritated the latter. However, the irony of it was that Eubank came from poorer circumstances than Benn, who revelled in his black, working-class credentials.

Benn made no secret of his contempt for Eubank. "*When he started calling me out on TV, my hatred for him became all-consuming,*" said Benn. He continued, "*What annoyed me most was the way he looked down his nose at everybody. Here was this black guy who thought he was a gentleman and different class to everybody else. All I thought about was doing a number on him.*"

The First Fight

Benn was under no obligation to take the fight against Eubank, who was not the mandatory challenger for his title. Indeed Eubank's camp was surprised and delighted that he agreed to it. Eubank's promoter, Barry Hearn, later recalled, "*Benn always had trouble against counterpunchers. He should have thought about it a bit more.*"

Benn would admit himself that Eubank's comments had goaded him into it, "*He lit the fuse real good, absolutely out-psyched me.*"

The challenger himself would have no doubt what would happen, claiming, "*Nigel Benn is the best puncher in the world, but he is up against a skillster. He will be exposed.*"

The mind games between the two camps continued until they entered the ring. Eubank liked to come out to Tina Turner's song '*Simply the Best*', so somebody from Benn's side arranged for the song to be turned off as he was halfway to the ring. Hearn tried to have the record put back on again, only to be prevented by two muscled security men.

When the opening bell rang, although Eubank caught Benn with an early blow, the opening rounds were largely devoid of intensity, with both men feeling the other out.

In the fourth round, though, the challenger was caught by a big right, which caused him to bite his tongue and swallow copious amounts of blood, something he hid from his corner, fearing a stoppage.

By the following round, Benn's eye had begun to swell and shut, and then Benn caught Eubank with a low blow that was judged accidental.

The contest was fairly even going into the eighth round, but then the momentum appeared to have shifted Benn's way when he caught Eubank with a left hook that knocked him down. Not only did Eubank get up, but he then responded with a flurry of blows that hurt the champion.

The end came just before the bell sounded for the end of the ninth round, when Eubank trapped his man in the corner against the ropes, repeatedly hitting him before the referee Richard Steele decided that he had seen enough.

Benn said, "*Only when Richard Steele stepped in and stopped that fight did I think I was going to lose. I would have rather lost to anyone else but him.*"

Steele himself described it as the "*Most dramatic fight I've ever refereed.*"

MICHAEL WATSON

Eubank made three defences of his title before relinquishing it to fight Michael Watson for the vacant WBO super middleweight title in September 1991, the man who had earlier beaten Benn.

Had fate been kinder, then history would still be talking about a Benn-Eubank-Watson rivalry, but what happened that night would profoundly affect the rest of Watson's life.

After ten rounds, Watson was ahead on all three judges' scorecards, and then he knocked Eubank down towards the end of the next round. Eubank got up and hit Watson with a savage right uppercut which caught Watson on the jaw and knocked his head and neck backwards into the ring ropes.

The fight was stopped in the 12th round, with Watson clearly suffering. Watson collapsed in his corner soon afterwards. There were no ambulances or paramedics on standby, and it was left to doctors wearing dinner jackets who were there to watch the fight, to attend to the stricken fighter.

It took 26 minutes for him to reach a hospital neurosurgical unit, and he spent 40 days in a coma, requiring six operations to remove a blood clot from the brain.

He spent a year in intensive care and rehab. It was followed by a further six years in a wheelchair and permanent brain damage. He later sued the British Boxing Board of Control for negligence and received £1 million in damages.

Eubank was profoundly affected by what happened to Watson and considered retiring on the spot, saying, "*I lost my finishing instinct in the ring – I couldn't finish fights any more. However, I needed to work, so I carried on and won most of my fights on decisions. And I blamed myself, after all, it was me who threw the punch.*"

Meanwhile, Benn had resumed his career, moving to super middleweight and challenging Mauro Galvano for the WBC title in Italy. Benn won by technical knock-out in the third round when a bad cut to Galvano brought proceedings to a premature end.

Following several successful defences, including a rematch with Galvano, he and Eubank met for what was meant to be a reunification match.

THE SECOND FIGHT

The second fight was watched by over 42,000 spectators at Old Trafford, Manchester, and by more than half a billion worldwide via pay-per-view. The fight was promoted by Don King, whose contract with the pair stipulated that both the winner and loser would join his stable of fighters afterwards.

Compared to the first fight, this was a cagier affair, with neither man able to seriously hurt the other.

The final round was the highlight, with both men geed up by their corners that they needed to win it to get the decision. The action ebbed back and forth and was later judged *"Round of the Year."*

Despite that, there was nothing to separate them at the end. One judge gave it to Eubank, another to Benn, and the third had the scores even. The fight was declared a draw, which meant Eubank got to keep his WBO title, and Benn his WBC version.

THE AFTERMATH

The pair never fought again, although there was talk of a highly lucrative bout at Wembley.

Instead, Benn, after several defences, met the WBC middleweight champion Gerald McClellan, who had been inviting comparisons with Mike Tyson because of the way that he would knock opponents out.

In a brutal fight, Benn stopped McClellan by technical knock-out in the 10th round, with the challenger unable to get up off his knees. He, too, collapsed in his corner, severely injured, and was rushed to hospital where doctors discovered a blood clot in his brain. He was left completely blind, partially deaf, and suffers even to this day from short-term memory loss.

Benn was never the same again, and soon after lost his title and was beaten twice by Irishman Steve Collins, who said that he wished he had been able to fight Benn at his peak. After their second fight, Benn retired from boxing altogether.

Eubank, too lost his title by split decision to Collins, and an attempt to move up to cruiserweight eventually ended in disappointment. He retired after being defeated in a rematch for the WBC world title.

LATER LIFE

Eubank has continued to maintain his reputation for eccentricity, purchasing lord of the manor rights in Brighton and going so far as to appoint a town crier. He has also appeared in several television shows, but his finances declined until he was declared bankrupt in 2009.

He was also arrested for anti-war activism after protesting about Britain's involvement in Iraq.

Benn has devoted most of his post-retirement life to charity work, helping children with life-threatening conditions. However, at age 55, after 23 years out of the ring, he announced a comeback, claiming that he wanted closure, feeling his career had not ended on the right note.

The British Boxing Board of Control refused to sanction his proposed fight against Sakio Bika. Still, although the British and Irish Boxing Authority approved it, the fight was called off after Benn suffered a shoulder injury.

EUBANK JR V BENN JR

Two of Benn's sons became boxers, with Conor Benn holding the Continental Welterweight title since 2018. Meanwhile, Eubank's son, Chris Jr, has held championships in two weight classes, middleweight and super middleweight.

They were scheduled to meet in London in October 2022, but the fight was cancelled after Conor Benn was found to have taken a banned substance. It has subsequently been blamed on excessive egg consumption, but Benn's licence remains suspended pending further investigation.

Promoters are still hopeful of the pair meeting in the future.

THE LEGACY

Even today, especially in Britain, sports fans of a certain generation vividly remember the fights and the hype surrounding them. As Hearn said, "*There was real antipathy and ill-will there. But what fights, what fights.*", whilst a later book chronicling their rivalry was called "*The Hate Game.*"

It should also be remembered that Eubank and Benn at least emerged relatively unscathed in their careers, whilst Watson and McClellan were not so lucky.

It is a reminder that, whilst boxing has been called the sport of kings, sometimes those kings can get severely damaged.

INTERESTING QUOTES

"I've tasted his blood and he has hurt me in ways you cannot imagine"

- Eubank on Benn

"It would give me a terrific sense of satisfaction to be the man who sent (Eubank) into retirement."

- Benn on Eubank

TYSON FURY V DEONTAY WILDER

The Gypsy King v The Bronze Bomber

Name	Tyson Luke Fury	Deontay Leshun Wilder
Height	6 feet 9 inches (206 com)	6 feet 7 inches (201 cm)
Weight	Heavyweight	Heavyweight
Hometown	Manchester, England	Tuscaloosa, Alabama
Nickname(s)	The Gypsy King	The Bronze Bomber
Overall Career Record	34 fights – 33 wins, 1 draw	46 fights – 43 wins, 2 losses, one draw
Head to head	2 wins, 1 draw, 0 losses	0 wins, 1 draw, 2 losses
Style	Orthodox	Orthodox
Recognition	WBA, WBO, IBF, IBO, The Ring Heavyweight champion, European and British heavyweight champion	WBC and The Ring heavyweight champion, WBC Continental heavyweight champion

In an era when the world heavyweight title had seemingly become devalued due to a diversity of belts and a series of champions who fought a series of no-hopers and virtual unknowns, the rivalry between Tyson Fury and Deontay Wilder was a throwback to an earlier age. They fought a trilogy of fights that will likely stand the test of time.

Both are prominent personalities outside the ring, with a flair for self-promotion. Whilst they have differing boxing styles – Fury is primarily a counter-puncher, whilst Wilder is more of a knock-out artist – they are both showmen who know how to play to the crowd.

In addition to their showmanship, both have attracted more than their fair share of controversy over the years.

In the end, it was the 'Gypsy King' who got the better of the 'Bronze Bomber', beating him in his own backyard. However, boxing was the ultimate winner, with many falling in love with the sport all over again.

TYSON FURY

Tyson Fury was born three months premature in Manchester in 1988, the son of traveller parents (hence his nickname). His father named him after Mike Tyson, the heavyweight champion at the time.

His family had a long history of boxing, with many of his relatives having professional careers, and Fury himself took up the sport at the age of ten. The following year he left school and went to work with his father and several of his brothers tarmacking roads.

His father trained him until 2011, when he was jailed for seriously hurting another man in a fight. One of his uncles then took over the role until he died, and then it was the turn of another uncle, Peter Fury, to take over the position. He had previously been jailed in the UK for his involvement in an amphetamine trafficking network.

Fury grew up boxing for England and Ireland as an amateur but missed the chance to represent Great Britain at the 2008 Olympics because of the one-fighter per-division rule. He also was unsuccessful in his application to fight for Ireland.

However, he did win the ABA super heavyweight title before turning professional.

Although not all his early displays were totally convincing, he won the British and Commonwealth titles in 2011 when he out-pointed the previously unbeaten Derek Chisora.

He later gave up those belts to further his ambition of fighting for a world title, beating the American Vinny Maddalone to win the Inter-Continental heavyweight title.

A series of fights among leading contenders followed before Fury beat Wladimir Klitschko, winning six versions of the world heavyweight title in the process.

He was, however, stripped of his IBF title because his clause with Klitschko included a mandatory rematch rather than fight the number one contender at the time.

Ultimately, the rematch did not happen, as Fury was stripped of his titles and suspended after a banned substance was found in his system – something he later blamed on eating unadulterated boar meat. He also suffered from mental health issues and experienced problems with alcohol and recreational drugs. It appeared as if his boxing career was over.

However, after nearly two years of inactivity, he successfully applied for his boxing licence to be reinstated and, after a couple of warm-up fights, announced his intention to fight Deontay Wilder for the WBC heavyweight title.

DEONTAY WILDER

Deontay Wilder was born in 1985 in Alabama and grew up with dreams of becoming either a professional basketball or an American football player. He did not begin boxing until he was 20, and by that time, he was married and a father to a daughter born with congenital problems. He decided to take up boxing full-time as it offered potentially the most lucrative rewards.

He enjoyed a successful amateur career, winning several prestigious championships. He was chosen to represent the US at the 2008 Olympics, settling for a bronze medal after losing his semi-final bout.

He turned professional the same year, acquiring the nickname 'The Bronze Bomber'. He embarked on a long winning streak, winning all his bouts by knock-out within the first four rounds.

Wilder worked his way up the ranks, becoming the number one challenger for the WBC heavyweight title, which he claimed by beating the Canadian Bermane Stiverne by unanimous decision, becoming the first American heavyweight champion since Shannon Briggs.

Several successful defences followed, including a rematch with Stiverne, which Wilder won via a first-round knock-out.

Finally, it was agreed that he would meet Fury for the first time.

THE ORIGINS OF THE RIVALRY

There had been talk about a fight between the two men for years before they actually met. In December 2015, just after Wilder had knocked out the Pole Artur Szpilka, Fury, sitting in the audience, climbed into the ring and called out Wilder in scenes bordering on the theatrical.

Fury told Wilder, "*There's only one Tyson Fury. What you got to say about that, Deontay?*"

Wilder replied, "*We all know, Fury, this is just an act, I ain't scared of nobody, and I'll come to your backyard for that fight, baby!*" Fury was not finished, though, saying, "*Any time, any place, anywhere, when you're ready, I'll fight you in your back garden like I done Klitschko. I'll beat you, you bum! You're a bum!*"

Wilder responded in kind, retorting, "*I don't play this, you can run around like you're a preacher and all that, but I promise you when you step in this ring, I will baptise you!*"

Everything was put on hold whilst Wilder fought his mandatory defences, and Fury struggled with his issues outside the ring. Instead, it was another British fighter that Wilder set his sights on beating, Anthony Joshua.

However, when the respective promoters of Joshua and Wilder could not agree on terms, attention turned to Fury again, who told the champion, "*I'll fight you in three seconds. Get your boss to send me the contract, and I'll show you how long it takes to sign it! If you wanna fight the best this country has ever had, knock on my door and see if the Gypsy King doesn't answer! The ball is in your court.*"

Wilder's response on social media was, "*There's one thing Tyson Fury has never had, and that's the WBC belt, and if he ever thinks about having it, he better wake up and apologises to me because he ain't never having it.*"

There was a certain sense of patriotism involved in the rivalry. Wilder considered himself an American champion fighting in his backyard to preserve what many considered the exclusive preserve of American sports fans – the world heavyweight title. Tyson was this interloper from across the pond, with a British-Irish heritage, determined to upset the established order.

THE FIRST FIGHT

The two legitimately stepped in the ring together for the first time at the Staples Center in Los Angeles in December 2018, with Fury spending most of the fight using his unorthodox stance to stay out of the way of some of Wilder's bigger shots.

The champion did get some joy in the fourth round when he caught the challenger with multiple stiff jabs, which caused his nose to bleed, but as the fight wore on, Fury began to exert himself more.

Wilder did put Fury down in the eighth round, but he had gained the upper hand by the time the bell rang for the 12th and final round. Wilder then caught Fury with a right-left combination that put Tyson down on his back again, and he, and most of those ringside, thought that the fight was over.

Much to the surprise of most, Fury beat the count and had the better of what remained of the action in the fight.

Fury later recalled his almost miraculous comeback from being virtuously unconscious, "*That last round is a Hollywood movie. If you saw that in Rocky, you would say, Pull back, Sylvester Stallone, you can't go that far.*"

The decision went to the judges, one of whom gave it to Wilder, another to Fury, and the third called it a draw.

It was officially called a draw, meaning Wilder had retained his title, a decision widely greeted by boos from many of the fans in the arena, who believed that Fury had won the fight.

Afterwards, Wilder said, "*I think with the two knockdowns, I definitely won the fight,*" whilst Fury believed, "*We're on away soil. I got knocked down twice, but I still believe I won that fight.*"

THE SECOND FIGHT

Talks about a rematch began almost immediately, although it would be another 15 months before the pair met again, this time in Las Vegas.

If the first fight had been a close contest, the second proved to be anything but. Almost from the opening bell, Fury looked to assert himself, jabbing Wilder at will and keeping out of range of some of his bigger punches. He got rewarded in the third round when he put Wilder down with a right hook to the temple. Wilder beat the count but was clearly discomfited with blood streaming from his left ear.

He hit the canvas twice in the fourth round, although the referee judged them as slips. However, he was knocked down again legitimately in the fifth round, and although he again beat the count, he was finding it difficult to defend himself by this time.

The fight was stopped midway through the seventh round when Fury trapped Wilder on the ropes and began pummeling him. Wilder's corner threw in the towel to stop their man from suffering any more punishment.

Afterwards, Wilder blamed his defeat on various factors, including that his water drink had been spiked, that his ring walk costume had been too heavy, and that Fury had scratched the blood out of his ears.

He also was critical of trainer Mark Breland for throwing in the towel, saying, "*No matter how you may love me or have that emotional feeling, don't make an emotional decision and do not ever throw that towel in because my pride is everything. I understand what it looks like, but when you have power like me, I am never out of a fight, no matter what the circumstances.*"

THE TRILOGY FIGHT

The second fight contract between the pair included a clause that, whoever lost it, could unilaterally invoke a third bout. Wilder lost no time activating the clause, vowing, "*We will rise again. We will regain the title. I will be back. We will hold our heads up high. Your king is in great spirit. We will rise like a phoenix from the ashes and regain the title. I'll see you in a few months. For the war has just begun.*"

The fight was tentatively scheduled for July that year, but then the Covid-19 pandemic intervened, and it would not be until October 2021 that the rematch finally happened, again in Las Vegas.

This time, Wilder started as the aggressor before Fury responded in the third round by catching Wilder with a right hook on the temple and following it up with a right uppercut which sent the challenger down. Wilder got up and scored a knockdown of his own next round, catching Fury with a straight left.

Fury got up, only to be knocked down again by a right hook.

Fury survived the rest of the round and gradually began to get on top as Wilder visibly began to tire. In the tenth round, Fury put Wilder down for the second time, and although he again beat the count, he was hanging on by this time.

The end came in the eleventh round, when, after a series of punches, Fury sent Wilder to the canvas again with a right hand that caught him flush on the temple. The referee decided that he had seen enough and stopped the fight.

Many commentators described it as one of the best heavyweight fights in recent history, and Fury considered it a fitting end to their trilogy.

Wilder, though, did not take defeat well, refusing to shake Fury's hand after the contest. In his post-fight interview, Fury reflected, "*I'm a sportsman. I went over to him to show some love and respect, and he didn't show it back. I will pray for him so that God will soften his heart.*"

A week later, though, Wilder was more magnanimous, saying, "*I would like to congratulate Tyson Fury for his victory and thank you for the great historical memories that will last forever.*"

THE AFTERMATH

Fury was ordered to defend his WBC title against mandatory number one challenger Dillian Whyte, which he did before a crowd of 100,000 at Wembley Stadium in London. The fight was stopped in the sixth round, with Whyte no longer able to defend himself.

After the fight, Fury announced his retirement, but it proved short-lived, and he returned to the right to fight and beat Derek Chisora for a third time at the Tottenham Hotspur stadium.

Fury has also become a well-known media personality in the UK, and a Netflix series is being made about him and his family. Wilder had his first fight in over a year since that final loss to Fury, knocking out Robert Helenius in the first round of their fight in Brooklyn.

THE LEGACY

The trilogy of fights has been credited with reviving heavyweight boxing. After their third contest in Las Vegas, promoter Bob Arum would claim that he had 'never seen a heavyweight fight as magnificent as this' during a career in boxing that had stretched back 57 years.

The fact that both were natural showmen helped add to the spectacle. Fury is known for his habit of impromptu singing after some of his fights, whilst Wilder, in particular, is known for his extravagant dress sense. Throw in some bad blood between the two into the equation, and all the ingredients are there for three classic encounters.

INTERESTING QUOTES

"Wilder can close that distance quick. He still poses the most imminent threat to me of all the heavyweights in the division, for sure. He's the only one with that single-punch power."

- Tyson Fury on Deontay Wilder

"This is no game. You get up in there, and you take some punches. You risk your life, and then let me see you talk then. That's why I don't respect people who criticize fighters"

- Deontay Wilder

MIKE TYSON V EVANDER HOLYFIELD

Iron Mike v The Real Deal

Name	Michael Gerard Tyson	Evander Holyfield
Height	5 feet 10 inches (178 cm)	6 feet 2.5 inches (197 com(
Weight	Heavyweight	Light heavyweight, cruiserweight, heavyweight
Hometown	Brooklyn, New York	Atmore, Alabama
Nickname(s)	Iron Mike, Kid Dynamite, The Baddest Man on the Planet	The Real Deal, The Warrior
Overall Career Record	58 fights, 50 wins, 6 losses, 2 no contests	57 fights, 44 wins, 10 losses, 2 draws, 1 no contest
Head to head	2 fights – Lost 2 (one by disqualification)	2 fights – Won 2 (one by disqualification)
Style	Orthodox	Orthodox
Recognition	WBA, WBC, IBF. The Ring Heavyweight champion	WBA, WBF, USBA, WBC Heavyweight champion, WBA and IBF Cruiserweight champion

The rivalry between Mike Tyson and Evander Holyfield is best remembered for what happened in their second fight in Las Vegas in 1997, which made headlines worldwide on the front and the back pages of newspapers.

It has gone down in history as the "bite fight", and the outcome saw Tyson disqualified and his boxing licence suspended.

Ironically, the two men later became close friends and even teamed up last year to market a range of edible cannabis sweets, referencing what happened in the ring that night in their promotion.

MIKE TYSON

"Iron Mike" Tyson was born in New York in 1966 into a low-income family and was brought up alone by his mother, the father having abandoned them. Growing up in neighbourhoods with a high crime rate, he often found himself involved in street fights, with older and bigger youths ridiculing him because he had a lisp and a high-pitched voice.

He became a petty criminal, and by age 13, he had been arrested 38 times. It was whilst he was at a juvenile detention centre that his boxing ability was first discovered by Bobby Stewart, a former boxer himself, who trained young Tyson for a while.

When his mother died aged 16, Tyson was left in the care of Cus D'Amato, a legendary trainer and boxing promoter, who subsequently became his legal guardian.

He would have an outstanding amateur career, winning gold at successive junior Olympics, culminating in him claiming heavyweight gold at the 1984 Olympic Games in Los Angeles.

The following year he turned professional and soon made a name for himself as an up-and-coming champion. However, some later blamed the death of D'Amato early in his career as the catalyst for some of the problems he was to experience both in and out of the ring.

After scoring a series of knock-out wins, Tyson was given his first title shot when he fought Trevor Berbick for the WBC heavyweight title. He won the fight by Technical Knock-Out (TKO) in the second round, becoming the youngest-ever heavyweight champion.

Tyson then won the unification series, fights designed to unify the heavyweight title, adding the WBA and IBF titles to the WBC belt he already held.

Acquiring the nickname "*The baddest man on the planet*", Tyson intimidated many opponents before they had even stepped in the ring with him, and there were some who considered him virtually unbeatable.

When he beat Leon Spinks, a man that some considered had a legitimate claim to be the heavyweight champion in his own right, after just 91 seconds of their fight, his reputation was cemented.

Personal problems outside the ring, however, then began to exact a toll, with a failing marriage and contractual issues. He accepted a fight against the barely known Buster Douglas in Tokyo. Still, he failed to train for it with his usual dedication, and, despite Douglas beginning the fight as a 42/1 underdog, he knocked Tyson out in the tenth round in what was one of the biggest sporting upsets of all time.

Tyson recovered from that loss with several quick wins. After two fights with Donovan 'Razor' Ruddock, he earned the right to be considered the number one contender to challenge Evander Holyfield for the world title.

They were initially scheduled to meet in November 1991, but Tyson's private life caught up with him before that could happen. He was arrested on charges of rape and subsequently convicted. He was sentenced to six years in prison and an additional four on probation.

After being paroled from jail, he resumed his boxing career and eventually regained his WBA and WBC belts before finally facing Holyfield.

EVANDER HOLYFIELD

Born in 1962 in Alabama, Holyfield began boxing at the age of seven but was a late developer by his own admission and would only grow to his full height in his early 20s.

Like Tyson, he fought at the Summer Olympics in 1984 as a light heavyweight but had to settle for bronze after being controversially disqualified in his semi-final bout.

He turned professional later that year as a light heavyweight before moving up to Cruiserweight, soon becoming the world champion in that division.

After several defences of his title, he set his sights on becoming world heavyweight champion and moved up a division again.

He soon became the number contender for the title that Tyson held at the time, but the champion swerved him to fight Buster Douglas, who beat Tyson in Tokyo causing a major upset.

Holyfield was Douglas' first title defence, but the challenger knocked him out to take his title.

Holyfield then beat former champion George Foreman, after which he was scheduled to meet Tyson for the first time.

Instead, he embarked on a trilogy of fights with Riddick Bowe – losing the first but winning the next two – before he and Tyson could finally meet in the ring.

THE ORIGINS OF THE RIVALRY

The rivalry was partly inspired by the fact that Holyfield had become the undisputed champion whilst Tyson had been in prison, and the former champion wanted his titles back.

They had also once been sparring partners, their sessions marked by ferocious punching from both men.

In addition, there was the issue of headbutts by Holyfield during the first fight. Although they were ruled accidental, the Tyson camp always believed that there was more to it than that. It would be used as a justification for what happened later, with Tyson effectively taking the law into his own hands (or teeth, as it transpired).

THE FIRST FIGHT

It was considered a complete mismatch when they finally met for the first time in November 1996. Tyson appeared to have lost none of his fighting ability whilst he had been inside – indeed, he seemed to have a renewed passion for the sport - whereas Holyfield, called by some the "Real Deal", appeared well past his best.

Fight promoter Don King was among those who considered Holyfield a washed-up fighter, whilst so concerned was the Nevada State Athletic Commission by what might happen to him against Tyson that they ordered Holyfield to undergo a full range of tests before sanctioning the fight.

Some bookmakers offered odds of 25/1 against Holyfield.

When the opening bell rang, it seemed that all the pre-fight predictions were about to come through as Tyson hit his opponent with a right hand that sent him staggering backwards. However, Holyfield confounded all expectations by fighting back, catching Tyson with sharp hooks and right uppercuts,

For a fighter who was meant to be past his prime, he showed surprising strength, and in the second round, he pinned Tyson against the ropes and hit him with several powerful, accurate shots. Tyson did not know how to deal with something that was not in the script.

Holyfield's dominance continued, although Tyson did win the fifth round when he finally managed to land some of his trademark left hook, left upper-cut combinations.

In the sixth round, Tyson was cut by a headbutt from Holyfield that the referee ruled was accidental.

Later in the same round, Holyfield caught his man with a left hook that dropped him to the canvass, the first time he had been knocked down since losing to Douglas.

As the next round drew to a close, the pair clashed heads again, and Tyson cried out in pain, but again it was ruled accidental.

The end of the tenth round proved decisive, with Holyfield catching Tyson with a shot to the temple that made his knees buckle. Rather than give himself time to recover, Tyson came forward and was hit by another huge right and would have been knocked down again but for the ropes getting in the way. A series of further blows went unanswered before the bell finally brought the round to a close.

Tyson came out for the eleventh round, but the referee soon stopped the fight, with Tyson virtually defenceless on the ropes. Tyson would later say, "*I don't remember that round. I got caught in something strange.*"

Holyfield would later reveal that he had followed his mother's advice, who had told him, "*Never lose against a reputation*", words that had encouraged him to go on the front foot against Tyson.

THE 'BITE FIGHT'

Seven months later, the pair met in a rematch in Las Vegas. Despite his defeat in their first contest, Tyson was still the slight favourite ahead of their second meeting, although he knew this was his last opportunity to reclaim his place at the very top of the sport.

Before the fight began, Tyson's camp objected to the appointment of Mitch Halpern to referee the fight again, believing that his leniency had allowed Holyfield to get away with several head butts in the first bout. Mills Lane was appointed instead.

Holyfield was on the front foot from the first bell again, forcing Tyson back and catching him with several telling blows. Tyson was becoming increasingly angry about Holyfield's use of his head, which opened a cut above his eye in the second round.

At the start of the third round, Tyson came out of his corner without his mouthpiece, and there was a delay whilst Lane insisted that he return to have it inserted.

When he came out again, Tyson launched a barrage of punches, and when Holyfield got him in a clinch later in the round, Tyson bit Holyfield on his right ear, tearing off a piece of cartilage from the top of the ear and spitting it onto the apron.

Holyfield cried out in pain, with blood pouring out of the wound. Tyson tried to continue, but the referee stopped the fight, unsure what to do next.

After consulting with the chair of the Nevada Athletic Commission, he decided to disqualify Tyson. However, after listening to the advice of the ringside doctors, he allowed the fight to continue.

The pair got in another clinch, and Tyson bit again, this time on Holyfield's left ear, just scarring it. This time the bite was not discovered immediately but was only noticed when the pair returned to their respective corners at the end of the round.

This time there would be no reprieve for Tyson, and he was disqualified. A furious Tyson tried to get to Holyfield and his trainer, who were quickly surrounded by security and escorted from the ring.

As he was leaving the ring, a fan threw a bottle of water at Tyson and his entourage, who broke into the crowd, making obscene gestures before being restrained.

Holyfield's version of events was that Tyson had bitten him because he knew he was going to get knocked out and preferred to lose by disqualification. Tyson, though, maintained that it was because of the headbutts, and if the referees did not give him justice, he would have to provide it for himself.

It was the first time in 50 years that a title fight in any division of boxing had ended with a disqualification.

The Aftermath

The Nevada State Athletic Commission decided to revoke Tyson's boxing licence and fined him US $3 million plus legal costs.

His licence was eventually restored, and he resumed his career. However, that was halted when he was given a fresh jail sentence for assaulting two motorists after a traffic accident.

He finally had the chance to fight again for a world title when he met Lennox Lewis in 2002, but Lewis dominated the fight and knocked him out in the eighth round.

His boxing career ended with him fighting several exhibition bouts in a world tour to raise money to help pay off some of his debts.

Holyfield would continue boxing for several years, but after a controversial draw with Lewis, he lost their second reunification bout. He did make history by beating John Ruiz to become the first man in history to be heavyweight champion four times. Still, his powers and strength began to fail, and, in the end, the New York Boxing Commission banned him from fighting in the State because of his diminishing skills.

He made a comeback and continued fighting until he was 47. He still considered himself a serious contender, but after three years of inactivity, he finally hung up his gloves.

Later Life

Tyson has continued to make money from personal appearances, published several autobiographies, and has also dabbled in wrestling. There have also been several other brushes with the law, and he served a brief prison sentence for drug-related issues, subsequently checking himself into rehab.

He has also made several cameo movie appearances. In addition, he has his own Foundation, which aims to give children from broken homes a fresh start in life.

Holyfield was a trainer to aspiring heavyweight boxer Zhilei Zhang for a while and also made a small fortune from personal appearances.

Despite that, like Tyson, he has had his own money issues, and, in 2012, despite having made over US $350 million from his boxing career, he was declared to be flat broke.

He has also faced allegations that he used steroids and performance-enhancing drugs during his boxing career. Holyfield has always denied this, and the claims have never been proven beyond a reasonable doubt.

Both men have been inducted into the World Boxing Hall of Fame.

THE LEGACY

Their rivalry has become defined by the 'Bite fight', which has assumed its place in the Sporting Hall of Infamy.

Despite that, Holyfield forgave Tyson for what happened in the ring that night, saying, "*Life's about forgiving. I had to let it go. Life goes on.*"

The pair would have a public reconciliation when they both appeared on the Oprah Winfrey show in 2009, Tyson telling the audience, "*I have great respect for him, and I wanted to beat him so bad. Even though people didn't give him the credit, I knew that [by] beating him, I would have conquered a giant. This is a beautiful guy. I just want you to know it's just been a pleasure ... being acquainted with you.*"

INTERESTING QUOTES

"*I overshadowed a lot of guys during my time, but he is inconceivably the most competitive human being I ever competed against. It's easy to overlook that because he's such a smooth, kind-hearted guy.*"

- Tyson on Evander Holyfield

"*I truly believe that if there wasn't a Mike Tyson people wouldn't think about how great I was. You are only as good as the people you fight.*"

- Holyfield on Mike Tyson

I wanted to say a HUGE thank you for buying this book. If you liked it, you can check out the other books in the series of Sports Rivalries.

If you enjoyed this book and would like to help other people find it too, please consider posting a little review at Amazon. Please do this for all the books you enjoy, because many authors depend on this kind of help to stay afloat and write their next book.

Printed in Great Britain
by Amazon

31635603R00083